NO WRINKLES ON THE SOUL

NO WRINKLES ON THE SOUL

A Book of Readings for Older Adults

RICHARD L. MORGAN

With a Foreword by Eugene C. Bianchi

UPPER ROOM BOOKS®
NASHVILLE

Cover Photo: Terry Livingstone
Cover Design: J. S. Loffbomm; *Book Design:* Thelma Whitworth

Enlarged-print Edition   First Printing: 2002

Library of Congress Cataloging-in-Publication Data

Morgan, Richard Lyon, 1929-
     No wrinkles on the soul : a book of readings for older adults /
Richard   L. Morgan ; with a foreword by Eugene C. Bianchi.
          p. cm.
     Originally published: 1990.
     Includes index.
     ISBN 0-8358-0972-2 (pbk.)
          1. Christian aged--Prayer-books and devotions--English. I. Title.
BV4580 .M572 2001
242'.65--cd21   2001046831

Printed in the United States of America

To older people
who taught me that the best is last
and to my grandsons,
Christopher William and Daniel Adam,
whose antics prevented me from
getting wrinkles on my soul.

*One cannot understand the meaning of
growing old without first coming to terms
with one's own humanity and with the
meaning of history; to age is to participate in
the humanity in which all persons share.*

John C. Morgan

Contents

Meditation Titles

Growing Older, But Not Old
The Potter's Purpose for Old Clay
Redirected, Not Retired
Life Begins at 75
Hoeing to the End of the Row
Claiming What Is Ours
God's Love Is like a Grandparent's
What Do We Leave Our Grandchildren?
She Had Many Grandchildren
Who Wants to Be Young Again?
Lamentations Went Out

Meditation Titles

Saying Goodbyes
Clearing Out the Clutter
Remembering to Forget
Holding On to Memories
Ironing with the Hottest Iron
Creating Your Own Space
Not Expecting Too Much
Balancing This Free Time
Avoiding Old-Age Temptations
Affirming Our Third Age

Meditation Titles

We Don't Want to Be a Burden
We Are Vulnerable

Old-Age Dropouts
We Triumph over Our Troubles
Old-Age Depression
Presbyopia and Presbycusis
Old Scars
Knocked Down, But Not Knocked Out!
Who Catches Us When We Fall?
Shut In, But Not Shut Out
The Relationship Heals

Meditation Titles

Not Needed Anymore
Where We Do Not Want to Go
A Displaced Person
Fears May Be Liars
No Substitute for Experience
The Age with Nothing to Do
On the Death of an Aged Friend
Acquainted with Grief
On the Death of a Parent
And the Life Everlasting

Meditation Titles

Learning to Pray in Old Age
She Did What She Could
No Halloween Masks in a Nursing Home
Golden Flecks amid the Ashes
Grandchildren Renew Our Lives
The Might of a Widow
Walk to Sunrise
Fragments Can Be Valuable
Our Disappointments,
   God's Appointments
The Beauty of a Mature Soul

Foreword

As we come to the end of the twentieth century, one more certainty can be added to those of death and taxes. This is the greatly expanding population of elderly people in the world's technologically developed countries. Planners of the future are just starting to cope with the graying of the West in terms of health care, housing, financing, and many other practical aspects of life.

Richard Morgan calls us to be creative about still another area of aging: spiritual satisfaction and growth. This easily readable book of meditations adds to a growing list of writings telling us that not by bread alone do we live.

These meditative reflections can be useful to anyone from middle age onward. But they seem to focus on issues that confront persons in the later phases of the aging process. The reader senses a deep awareness of the fragilities and limitations that are more pronounced in the final years of the Third Age. Morgan's honesty about certain losses and their attendant pain becomes a gift to us. We are pulled away from the pleasant advertising that sells retirement communities. We are led beyond the pretty pictures of trouble-free aging to experience the heart of the matter. We need to journey to such rock-bottom issues if we are to construct an enduring house for aging well. It has been said that we must look at the worst in order to contemplate the best.

George Bernard Shaw asserted that youth is wasted on the young. But I'm afraid we could say today that aging is wasted on the elderly. So much talent, skill, and wisdom is lost to society at large when aging persons are ignored or rejected. But it is even sadder when they see themselves as useless and lacking in value to others. Morgan's meditations may take us into negativities of aging, but it is for the purpose of tapping and channeling the great gifts of the elderly for the world. Some older people will exercise these abilities on larger social issues of justice, peace, ecology, and human rights. But others will make their contributions in quiet and personal ways with children, the sick, and the isolated. However we use the talents purified in the crucible of aging, Morgan wants us to "hoe to the end of the row," not to lie down with self–pity in the middle of the furrow.

But such perseverance to the end requires spiritual resources. Morgan's book is of universal appeal, although he leans heavily on the biblical tradition for sustenance. That tradition is rich with powerful insights into various stages of the life cycle, and it contains an accumulated wisdom of faith communities over millenia of human experience.

These short meditations lend themselves nicely to the still busy life-styles of many aging persons. They can be used for a brief spiritual reading in the morning or perhaps at a transitional moment during the day. However we use them, they can stir up the gift of God within us. As we struggle with the new problems of the graying of the West on the cusp of the twenty-first century, we need to be enabled to live fully by the spiritual wisdom of our heritage. Science and technology will be vitally necessary to meet the new challenges of aging populations. But as the Bible reminds us, without spiritual vision, the people will perish.

Eugene C. Bianchi
author of *Aging as
a Spiritual Journey*

Preface

It struck me like lightning! I am getting older. First, the youthful waitress said, "Of course you want the senior citizen's discount." (Did I really look *that* old?) And then a gentleman, obviously much older than I, tapped me on the shoulder and said, "Old-timer, you left your lights on!" Believe me, I had entered the "gray" world.

As I enter my sixty-second year, I am all too aware of the need for spiritual direction. The old clichés and worn-out platitudes don't help. Older people are hungry for the eternal word.

This anthology on aging grew out of my own need and my perception of the needs of countless older adults—those living in their own homes, in nursing homes, retirement villages, and senior centers. With more time on our hands, we want to grow spiritually and to age gracefully. I trust these meditations and reflections will make your aging less fearful and more graceful.

My thanks go to a number of people at Upper Room Books who made this publication possible: to Jill Reddig who first approved of the uniqueness of this book; and to Glenda Webb, Sarah Linn, Lynne Deming, and George Graham, who shared the task of producing the final version of the manuscript and made "the rough places a plain."

Life Begins Every Day

I felt more alive as my seventy-fourth birthday rolled by than I had when I was young. Increasingly, I saw new possibilities, uninhibited confidence surged in me again. I was my own woman—in some ways more than ever before.

Sarah–Patton Boyle

1

So we do not lose heart. Though our outer nature is wasting away, our inner nature is being renewed every day.

2 Corinthians 4:16 (RSV)

READ FOR REFLECTION

One of the more interesting discoveries of recent gerontology is that each person is in reality three different ages at once: the *chronological* age, which is determined by the number of years [one] has lived; the *biological* age, which is determined by the condition and state of [the] body; and finally, the *psychological* age, which is measured by how old a person feels and acts.

It is of great importance for an aging person to avoid a narrow, fatalistic view that makes the age marked by the calendar, the chronological age, the norm for one's feeling and acting. Some people age fast biologically precisely because they *feel* old. On the other hand, we have all met octogenarians who felt younger at heart than many people only half their age.

ALFONS DEEKEN

MEDITATION

Growing Older, But Not Old

The word *old* still may carry a lot of negative images in people's minds. For many, to be old stirs images of senility, sickness, and sleeplessness—of being relegated to the sidelines of life. Some older people deny their aging and cling to their lost youth like young chicks cling to their shells. But nothing can stop the aging process. A person begins to age at the moment of birth.

Have you ever considered that it is possible to grow *older*, but never *old*? As we grow older, we have to cope with slowed-down reflexes, weaker vision, a slower step, or hearing impairment. "Our outer nature is wasting away." All the cosmetics and beauty creams cannot hide the wrinkles and liver spots. Didn't Jesus say, "Who of you by worrying can add a single hour to his life?" (Matt. 6:27, NIV)

Yes, we grow older, but age is a state of mind. "Our inner nature is being renewed every day." As long as we keep our hopes and dreams alive, as long as we stay involved in life, our spirits will be renewed. There should be no wrinkles on the soul.

The preacher at a wedding made a mistake when he gave the groom his wedding vows. He asked, "Will you love, honor, and obey her as long as you last?" His error became a moment of truth for all older people. We should live as long as we last. We may grow *older*, but let us never grow *old*.

PRAYER

Dear Creator God, the years come and go, and we do age. We cannot deny it or even wish to find a fountain of youth. What we pray is that we may stay vital and creative as long as we last. In your name. *Amen.*

2

 The vessel he was making of clay was spoiled in the potter's hand, and he reworked it into another vessel, as it seemed good to the potter to do.

Jeremiah 18:4 (RSV)

READ FOR REFLECTION

Jeremiah went down to the potter's house with heavy heart. The nation, Judah, was headed for ruin. Its repeated refusals to be faithful to the covenant ensured its doom. Like the old, marred clay in the potter's house, Israel seemed beyond redemption. But a miracle of sorts happened. The potter did not discard the old clay, but began to rework it, redirect it on [the potter's] wheel. . . .

The potter did not discard the old clay. With great patience and love he gave it back its dignity and restored its pride. What greater gift can we give God than to do that for our older people? What greater miracle for the church than to see its older people mobilized and energized for action? What greater way to love ourselves, who some day, if not now, will be old?

RICHARD L. MORGAN

MEDITATION

The Potter's Purpose for Old Clay

So often when we mature adults look back on our lives, we have many regrets, if not remorse. *If only*— those two words can bite into our souls and torment our nights. Some things just didn't turn out as we hoped they would. We have known some hard disappointments and broken dreams. Too often we learned to live with second-bests.

At the time Jeremiah spoke the words of today's scripture to the people of Israel, they felt like discarded old clay. They had not shaped up the way Yahweh had intended; the bright hopes of being God's covenant community had been shattered by their stubborn refusals.

But God still had a plan for the old clay. With infinite patience and kindness, God reworked the old clay until it took on a new and more beautiful shape. And from that reshaped clay came hope for the future.

We need to take heart and realize that when we are in God's hands, we don't have to surrender to despair. All our sins are forgiven by grace; and somehow, in the mysteries of God's providence, even our failures can be redeemed.

PRAYER

Lord, we may be old clay, but we can still be reworked. We know you never discard anyone. Show us, this day, what new purpose you have for our lives. *Amen.*

3

 At the age of fifty, they must retire from their regular service and work no longer. They may assist their brothers in performing their duties at the Tent of Meeting, but they themselves must not do the work.

Numbers 8:25-26 (NIV)

READ FOR REFLECTION

A psychologist said: "In retirement you need to face yourself afresh. Have the courage to explore some other aspect of yourself. Try to find something you have left undone, some interest that got covered through the years. Prove to yourself that you still have reserves, mental and physical."

Retirement might be life's strictest judge. It makes you aware of what you are worth to yourself by revealing what you have been becoming all of those years. If you have not become "somebody" you will not accept responsibility for the tenor of your life, but will expect that relatives, or the government, or some organization will shape your life to your liking. What you really need is to admit that you are responsible for your own happiness and misery, that you create your heavens and hells, and are the architect of your fate.

EDWARD FISCHER

24

MEDITATION
Redirected, Not Retired

The word *retirement* can be misleading. For some, retirement connotes a stop sign or a rocking chair. Perhaps the word *redirection* is a better one. That means a new beginning for the best twenty years of our lives.

The Levites retired from active ministry at age fifty, but that did not mean complete inactivity. They began "second careers" in assisting, advising, ministering to their fellow Levites in the tent of the meeting. Their retirement seems to have included becoming teachers and advisors to the younger men.

Perhaps we should stop using the word *retirement* with its often negative connotations, and use instead the concept of *freedom*. Freedom to read, to interact socially, to change one's life-style, to find new priorities. In retirement we can have freedom to explore our fantasies and dreams, and even our absurd ideas.

Retirement is redirection. In retirement we may *do* a bit less so that we can *be* who we are. We may slow down, but we can be as active and involved as we ever were. Retirement is just another station on life's journey as we change gears and move on.

PRAYER ━━━━━━━━━━━━━━━━━━━━━━━━━━━━━━

Help us, O God, to see retirement as filled with opportunity, not as a curse. As we slow down from our frantic pace, point us to peace and service. *Amen.*

4

 So Abram went, as the Lord had told him. . . . Abram was seventy-five years old when he departed from Haran.

Genesis 12:4 (RSV)

READ FOR REFLECTION

When, therefore, in our own time we see a man or woman in the later years who maintains the questing spirit, and who does so with courage and resourcefulness in a wide variety of circumstances, many of them terribly, even tragically adverse, such a man or woman may well be described as Ulyssean. The quest, the courage, and the resourcefulness may be exhibited on a human stage of immense proportions or in total solitariness and obscurity. It is not the time or the location but the quality of the life being lived that creates the Ulyssean Adult.

JOHN A. B. McLEISH

MEDITATION
Life Begins at 75

Surely Abram was not seventy-five years old when God called him to leave his home and make that incredible journey of faith! Biblical time must have been different from ours, and this was just a mid–life crisis.

Why can't we accept the fact that God can and does use older people? God's wisdom does not discount the rich talents of older people. God knew that Abram had the potential for greatness at age seventy-five!

Abram was like the legendary Ulysses, who came home from the Trojan wars after a long struggle and tried to settle down. But the old warrior was not content to sit. Instead, Ulysses looked for some "work of noble note" yet to be done. Some call older people like this Ulyssean adults. Abram was one.

Another was an old woman from eastern Kentucky named Granny Sukie. Sharon R. Curtin tells us that Granny, over a hundred years old, once told her:

> The last years of a woman's life should be spent in trying to settle what's inside. Early on a woman is so filled with things outside—her looks and her husband, and her children and her home—that she never has a chance to be just private. I've had more private time, now, than I need; but I value these years just the same.

We never know what adventures lie ahead when we move out in faith.

PRAYER ━━━━━━━━━━━━━━━━━━━━━━━━━━━━

Call us, O awesome God, to some incredible journey of faith in our own lives. We are not content to mark the end of our days in inactivity. We want to be challenged, to have something useful to do. *Amen.*

5

 Jesus said to him, "No one who puts his hand to the plow and looks back is fit for the kingdom of God."

Luke 9:62 (RSV)

READ FOR REFLECTION

At any time, from infancy to old age, crises may arise in the individual life. In any one of a myriad combinations of outward and inward events, one finds [one]self in circumstances where [one] feels the propulsion to pass over some sort of Jordan and enter upon some new level of responsibility and recompense. And yet this new step forward is a step into the unknown, peopled with dangerous creatures of fact, as truly as with menacing creations of fantasy. The stage one has already reached in growth is good, though not yet fully satisfying. In that case is it better to bear the ills we know, or fly to others that we know not of? So the motive of growth is met by the motive of shrinking back. In that time of conflict, we have come to crisis, whether we are one year old, or three score years and ten.

LEWIS J. SHERRILL

MEDITATION

Hoeing to the End of the Row

Some years ago I was called to the bedside of one of my "adopted fathers," a country doctor whom I had known in a previous parish. Although weakened by age, he had served his church as an elder for over sixty years and had worked tirelessly in service to the community.

We reminisced about those bygone days. He told me stories I will never forget, and we both chuckled as we recalled some of his funniest experiences. I left the hospital with a mixture of sadness and joy. I was sad because the truth of those depressing words from "O God, Our Help in Ages Past" grabbed me: "Time, like an ever rolling stream, bears all who breathe away; / they fly forgotten, as a dream dies at the opening day."

But I could rejoice too because I knew there was something about him, something about his ministry of healing and something about our relationship which that ever-rolling stream could not wash away. Although his body was frail, his spirit was as vital as ever, and I knew the source of that vitality was Jesus Christ.

At his funeral, I focused on Jesus' words about keeping our hand to the plow of the kingdom, and I said of him, "He hoed to the end of the row." He never shrank back from his responsibilities. He kept the faith until the end.

PREYER

PRAYER

O God the Spirit, fill our minds at this moment with the memory of an older person whose witness we recall. May his or her life serve as an inspiration to us, that we may persevere until the fever of this life is past, and we are at home with you. *Amen.*

6

 And now, lo, I am this day eighty-five years old.
I am still as strong to this day as I was in the day
that Moses sent me; . . . So now give me this hill
country of which the Lord spoke on that day.

Joshua 14:10-11, 12 (RSV)

READ FOR REFLECTION

We are not "senior citizens" or "golden-agers." We are
the elders, the experienced ones; we are maturing,
growing adults responsible for the survival of our society. We are not wrinkled babies, succumbing to trivial,
purposeless waste of our years and our time.

We are a new breed of old people. There are more of us
alive today than at any other time in history. We are
better educated, healthier, with more at stake in this
society. We are redefining goals, taking stock of our
skills and experience, looking to the future.

Erik Erikson speaks of old age as "a time of integrity," of
absolute honesty in an age that has lost its way, in terms
of deception, double-dealing, corruption in high and
low places. Old age is also a time of great fulfillment—
personal fulfillment, when all the loose ends of life can
be gathered together.

MAGGIE KUHN

MEDITATION

Claiming What Is Ours

After the Israelites had conquered the land, eighty-five-year-old Caleb went to his former colleague Joshua and claimed the promised hill country. The gift of the land was designed to show how God keeps promises to those who are faithful. Caleb, as an older person, claimed his rights.

The following words were spoken by an ancient writer a century before the birth of Christ:

Old age is worthy when it defends itself, when it asserts its rights, is subservient to none, and to the last breath, rules over its own domain.

Sometimes we older people are afraid to assert ourselves. But we do need to claim our legitimate rights without anger or apology. Thus we show that we respect ourselves and that we have the power to choose our own activities, rather than passively letting others control us.

Older people are people with rights. It is time for us, like Caleb, to learn to be assertive on our own behalf.

PRAYER

Redeemer God who strengthens us, help us as older people to stand up for ourselves, lest we fall for anything. Give us the grace not to be angry with others or to let others control us. Help us to be our own persons. *Amen.*

7

As a father pities his children,
  so the Lord pities those who fear him.
For he knows our frame;
  he remembers we are dust.
                    Psalm 103:13-14 (RSV)

READ FOR REFLECTION

We limit God when we cast doubts upon [God's] love, because [this] love is like any other love: it can always be measured by the amount it is ready to give. And God gave everything, because none of us is ever beyond the scope of [God's] love. John Henry Jowett, the great English Congregationalist minister, said at the close of his life, "I proclaimed always that everyone is in the love grip of the eternal." And many of us found that when life seemed to have tumbled in and we were at the very edge of things the love of God was all we had left and all we needed to have anyway. Shall we presume then to limit God?

DONALD MACLEOD

MEDITATION

God's Love Is like a Grandparent's

Throughout the ages we have tried to describe God's love with different idioms. Did you ever think of God's love as being like a grandparent's love? Oh, I don't mean some "sweet, old grandfather in the sky," but God's love *is* like a grandparent's love.

Like our grandparents who loved us before we were born, God has loved us from eternity. As the hymn "I Sought the Lord" puts it so well, "For thou wert long before-hand with my soul; / Always thou lovedst me."

Grandparents often bring little gifts to their grand-children; and yet, for a while, the grandchildren may be too young to realize the donors of these gifts. Only later do they realize that that special Teddy or that nice book came from Grandpa or Grandma. In the same way God has surrounded us with countless gifts of love, and sometimes we are unaware of those blessings.

> Who, from our mothers' arms, has blessed us on
> our way with countless gifts of love,
> and still is ours today.
>
> (from the hymn "Now Thank We All Our God")

Any of us who have been grandparents know that we are available in a special way to our grandchildren. We are like the lady who said, "If I had known what a joy my grandchildren were, I would have had them first." In a unique way, God's love is always available for us. Like the father of the prodigal son, God waits for our return with outstretched arms of love and forgiveness.

PRAYER ━━━━━━━━━━━━━━━━━━━━━━━

Dear Grandfather God, how much you love us! You hold us in your arms when we are scared or uncertain. We know your love can make everything right. Thank you. *Amen.*

8

 By faith Jacob, when he was dying, blessed each of Joseph's sons, and worshiped as he leaned on top of his staff.

Hebrews 11:21 (NIV)

READ FOR REFLECTION

I think it is worthwhile to think back to your own family and the kinds of blessings that occurred there. Who was it in your family who blessed you? Who was it who gave you that sparkle in their eye, who took delight in you, so that you really knew that you were a beloved son or daughter in whom they were well pleased? Who was it who blessed you? Mother? Father? Maybe an older brother or sister, or aunt or uncle? Maybe even a neighbor or teacher or pastor? I know that for me, when I was very young and my parents were pressuring me to be perfect, it was my grandfather who simply liked me. I still think of that as one of the most important influences in my life. . . .

What the blessing does is to set the child free to be his [or her] own person. It satisfies a kind of deep yearning in a person that has to be met if [one] is to get beyond that and really be free to be [oneself]. Once that quest is finished, there is a new freedom to find one's place in the world.

HENRY T. CLOSE

MEDITATION
What Do We Leave Our Grandchildren?

He clutched the little yellow flower in his tiny fist. As we began our walk along that long mountain trail, my grandson on his father's back, I put a small flower in his hand, and he smiled and said, "Wower." All afternoon he held that flower. When we returned to the parking lot, his mother said, "We'll have to preserve Grandpa's flower."

What do we leave our grandchildren? Manasseh and Ephraim, the grandchildren of Jacob, sat on their grandfather's knee, symbolizing their acceptance into the family. He showered such a blessing on them that they were considered his own sons (Gen. 48:5, NIV). This acceptance meant that these grandsons had the blessing of a freeing love which gave them room to grow.

Are the materialistic things of life all that we leave our grandchildren—savings for college, precious property, treasured possessions? Or can we leave our grandchildren a better world, symbolized by a flower? Can we leave them real peace on earth and a future unmarred by nuclear threats or a polluted environment? What better gift than our blessing, our total acceptance, our unending love?

PRAYER ━━━━━━━━━━━━━━━━━━━━━━━━━━━━━━

Source of blessing, you have blessed us all our days. May we show our gratitude by the way we bless our grandchildren, freeing them to be their own special persons. *Amen.*

9

> Coming up to them at that very moment, she gave thanks to God and spoke about the child.
>
> Luke 2:38 (NIV)

READ FOR REFLECTION

Cartwright was whispering to Merivale. "Poor old chap—must have lived a lonely sort of life, all by himself."

. . . .

"Pity. Pity he never had any children."

. . . .

[Chips replies] "Yes—umph—I have," he added, with quavering merriment. "Thousands of 'em . . . thousands of 'em . . . and all boys."

JAMES HILTON, *Goodbye Mr. Chips*

Very young children and very old children also seem to be in touch with something that the rest of the pack has lost track of. There is something bright and still about them at their best, like the sun before breakfast. Both the old and the young get scared sometimes about what lies ahead of them, and with good reason, but you can't help feeling that whatever inner goldenness they're in touch with will see them through in the end.

FREDERICK BUECHNER

MEDITATION

She Had Many Grandchildren

She had been a widow for several years and had never had children or grandchildren. Some felt she lived a rather isolated life, surrounded by her mementos of the past and dependent on her telephone for contact with others. But she had many "grandchildren." Pictures of adorable children filled her living room.

She had adopted several children at a nearby children's home. She was always sending cards and gifts to "my grandchildren" in her church. As a former teacher, she kept in touch with the children of her former students. She realized the hope that exists in the next generation.

In the scripture reading Anna, an older woman, had been a widow for many years. After seven years of marriage, she had been left a young widow in an age when women had few ways of caring for themselves. But her grief gave way to a new spiritual rebirth.

Many who saw Jesus saw only another peasant baby, but Anna's heart was receptive. She recognized Jesus as God's promised Messiah, and she spoke about him to all who hoped for the redemption of Israel.

There are many "foster grandparents" who see the infinite possibilities in little children and who love them as if they were their own.

PRAYER

For all the adopted grandparents who have blessed our lives, we thank you, God. For all the adopted grandchildren whom we have loved, whose lives have touched ours, we will always be grateful, dear Lord. *Amen.*

10

 Wisdom is with the aged;
and understanding in length of days.
Job 12:12 (RSV)

READ FOR REFLECTION

Would I wish to be 'young' again? No, for I have learned too much to wish to lose it. It would be like failing to pass a grade in school. I have reached an honorable position in life, because I am old and no longer young. I am a far more valuable person today than I was 50 years ago, or 40 years ago, or 30, 20, or even 10. I HAVE LEARNED SO MUCH SINCE I WAS 70! . . . This, I suppose, is because I have perfected my techniques, so that I no longer waste time in learning how to do what I have to do.

PEARL S. BUCK

MEDITATION

Who Wants to Be Young Again?

One question we often ask ourselves at any age is, "If I had to do it all over again, would I have done anything differently?" Would you really want to go back and live life over again? At times we seem to envy the young, who seem to have life before them and are not burdened with remorse and regrets.

To be honest, I don't envy the young. They have so much to learn, so many rough roads to walk, so many disappointments to overcome. Older people have an advantage, because we have lived through so much already and have grown wiser through it all.

The philosopher George Santayana once said, "Nothing is inherently and invincibly young except spirit. And spirit can enter a human being perhaps better in the quiet of old age and dwell there more undisturbed than in the turmoil of adventure." A sense of peace comes when we accept our lives as a gift to the world. With Paul we can affirm, "By the grace of God, I am what I am" (1 Cor. 15:10, RSV).

We have grown through our experiences; we have matured through our struggles. Paul was right when he said, "We rejoice in our sufferings, knowing that suffering produces endurance, and endurance produces character, and character produces hope" (Rom. 5:3-4, RSV). That is why we would not want to go back. Rather, we would hear what God said through Moses to the children of Israel, "Tell the people of Israel to go forward" (Exod. 14:15, RSV).

PRAYER ━━━━━━━━━━━━━━━━━━━━━━━━━━

Dear Lord, we would not waste time pining for our youth, or wish we could relive the years. No, we celebrate our age, and affirm our experience. *Amen.*

39

11

 For everything there is a season, . . .
a time to weep, and a time to laugh;
a time to mourn, and a time to dance.

Ecclesiastes 3:1, 4 (RSV)

READ FOR REFLECTION

Is it possible for the elderly to refind the wisdom of the child in a second playfulness? To care for the elderly means to play with the elderly in the hope that by playing together we will remind each other that dancing is more human than rushing, singing more human than shouting orders, poetry more human than *The Wall Street Journal*, and prayers more human than tactful conversations. To play with the elderly is to recapture the truth that what we are is more important than what we achieve. It is not a regression to a childish state, but a progression to a second innocence in which the acquired skills and insights of adulthood are fully integrated. This second innocence can lead us to the mature and critical realization that celebration is the most human response to life. This is of utmost importance in our worship. When worship is no longer play and when all gestures and words have become deadly serious, then we have made God into another demanding boss and have forgotten that [God] is a loving father who calls us children and not rivals, friends and not slaves.

HENRI J. M. NOUWEN

MEDITATION

Lamentations Went Out

A little boy accompanied his father, a preacher, to a country church. Sixty-six red lights were burning over the pulpit, one for every book of the Bible. During the sermon, the boy became quite excited. Later when he was asked why he behaved in such a way, he replied, "Daddy, you couldn't see, but Lamentations went out."

It is time for lamentations to go out for older people. There is a time to weep, but also a time to laugh; a time to mourn, but also a time to dance.

We are still caught in the grips of the old Puritan work ethic, which considers play sinful. Even when we retire from the work force, we feel pangs of guilt when we play. Zechariah's vision of the future welfare of Jerusalem finds old men and women sitting in the streets watching many children playing. "Once again men and women of ripe old age will sit in the streets of Jerusalem, each with cane in hand because of his age. The city streets will be filled with boys and girls playing there" (Zech. 8:4-5, NIV).

Jesus took time to play. He even used some of the children's games in the marketplace to teach a lesson that some people are like children who play marriage or funeral (see Matt. 11:16-19; Luke 7:31-34). The ancient rabbis had a saying that when a funeral procession and a wedding procession met at an intersection, the funeral procession had to give way. There is a time to play and dance. Let's not feel guilty but, instead, enjoy those moments.

PRAYER ━━━━━━━━━━━━━━━━━━━━━━━━━━━━━

Father, help us to release the "little child" in us which is spontaneous and full of fun. Give us a healthy sense of humor and the ability to play.   *Amen.*

Tasks of Aging

It takes a long time to become young.

Pablo Picasso

12

 Jesus said to her, "Do not hold on to me."
John 20:17 (NIV)

READ FOR REFLECTION

At every point in the human journey we find that we have to let go in order to move forward; and letting go means dying a little. In the process we are being created anew, awakened afresh to the source of our being. Aging is a paradox, the unity of apparent contradictions. Jesus challenges his followers with this paradox when he says, "For anyone who wants to save his life will lose it; but anyone who loses his life for my sake will find it" (Mt. 6:25). Emptiness can somehow be fullness, weakness can be strength, and dying can lead to new life. A spirituality of aging must help us find a way to turn losses into gains, to learn how the stripping process which often accompanies aging can be a gradual entrance into freedom and new life, how, in fact, aging can be winter grace.

Winter is a season of some very real losses. The flowers of springtime are gone; leaves fall. Trees stand bare and revealed. But from these losses there are gifts to be had.

KATHLEEN R. FISCHER

MEDITATION

Saying Goodbyes

Integral to life are our hellos and goodbyes. We have to say goodbye to the old in order to say hello to the new. Healthy people can say their goodbyes and move on; unhealthy people put it off and even work hard to deny their goodbyes.

Mary Magdalene had to learn to say goodbye to the Jesus she loved in this life so she could say hello to a new dimension of his presence. She could *not* hold on to the Jesus of history. Only when she could say goodbye could she move on in her faith story.

At any age people say goodbyes. But as we grow older, it seems we have to say a lot of goodbyes. We say goodbye to a friend who moves to another city to live with a son, or goodbye to a dear friend who has died. If we are ill for a time, we say goodbye to a certain degree of independence. It is natural to experience some grief over each of these.

But we can find ways to turn these losses into gains. The "goodbyes" of old age can become the "hellos" of a new life. We can learn to be centered on God's work in our lives. We can gain perspective and a deeper insight into the true meaning of everything. The psalmist called it "a heart of wisdom" (Psalm 90:12, RSV). So, "Goodbye and hello!"

PRAYER

Loving God, it is hard to say goodbye to what and whom we love; we do get attached to people and things in this life. But give us your grace to let go of what we need to let go of so that we may grow in your love. *Amen.*

45

13

 He said to them, "Take heed and beware of covetousness; for one's life does not consist in the abundance of things he possesses."

Luke 12:15 (NKJV)

READ FOR REFLECTION

In the last century an American tourist visited the renowned Polish Rabbi Hofetz Chaim. The tourist was amazed to find the Rabbi's home only a simple room, filled with books, a table, and a bench. "Rabbi," he asked. "Where is your furniture?"

"Where is yours?" asked the Rabbi.

"Mine?" asked the puzzled American. "But I'm only a visitor here. I'm only passing through."

"So am I," replied the Rabbi.

JAMES A. THORSON and THOMAS C. COOK, JR.

One of the things we may have to learn to do as we move into the later years is to simplify our lives by focusing on the essentials and getting rid of the clutter. This may mean having a garage sale or giving away many of the things that become a nuisance to care for. It may mean moving from a large place to a smaller place that is more manageable in terms of income and strength. It may mean resigning from some of the organizations and giving up some of the projects that drain our energy. In our society it is easy to accumulate too many things and to belong to too many groups. . . . Life is more than things; the self is larger than what we possess of material goods.

PAUL B. MAVES

MEDITATION

Clearing Out the Clutter

Many of us at some time in our lives have to deal with what someone has called the "attic syndrome," meaning, what will we do with all those things we have accumulated throughout the years? G. Stanley Hall talks about going through his house, after he retired, and getting rid of everything he did not want. He called this process "getting rid of waste material."

The later years of life may be the time to clear out the clutter. These may be a time to give things away—unneeded things to friends or charities, and special items to special people. We realize that too much clutter prevents us from centering on life's priorities instead of on life's incidentals.

We need to realize that dejunking life has spiritual value. Jesus told his disciples as they embarked on their first missionary journey, "Take nothing for your journey" (Luke 9:3, rsv). Travel light. Don't be encumbered with possessions and things. Our true life consists not of "the abundance of possessions," but of who we are, our character.

PRAYER ━━━━━━━━━━━━━━━━━━━━━━━━━

Help us, dear God, to be like the widow of the Gospels, who gave everything she had for the kingdom. May we be so wise that we realize that all we take out of this life are spiritual values and the person we have become. *Amen.*

14

 Joseph called the name of the first-born Manasseh, "For," he said, "God has made me forget
all my hardship."

Genesis 41:51 (RSV)

READ FOR REFLECTION

The fear of forgetting and the need to remember both
mark the later years of life. This fear and need spring
from the same truth. Memory is more than a resource
for efficient living or a reservoir of colorful and enter-
taining stories. Memory enables us to hold fast to our
identity and shape it in new ways. Beneath the an-
noyance we experience at not being able to recall names
and dates or find our glasses is the nagging fear that
some part of us is slipping away. On the other hand,
remembering events and people from our past lets us
claim and share ourselves. Somewhere within us still
lives the girl of nine racing across the grass in the sum-
mer sunshine, the young man finding his way in first
friendships, the wife receiving the news of her husband's fatal heart attack. We do not merely *have* these
memories; we *are* these memories.

KATHLEEN R. FISCHER

MEDITATION

Remembering to Forget

Remembering to forget. These may sound like strange words, for older adults seem to have a constant fear of forgetting. Many of us become irritated when we cannot remember names or dates, or where we put our glasses, or how much medicine we took today. Sometimes forgetfulness makes us feel as if we are losing our minds. So, what does "remembering to forget" mean?

Joseph had a lot of bitter memories: the hatred and jealousy of his brothers, their treacherous betrayal, and their murderous act of selling him into Egypt. But he had learned the grace of forgiveness. He even named one of his sons Manasseh, "God has made me forget."

We need to remember to forget old wounds from the past. Old resentments and bitterness need to be discarded, so that we can face life and death with a clear conscience. Sometimes people suffer from depression because they hold on to old resentments. This kind of depression may even be repressed anger.

We need to forgive ourselves. No doubt the brothers of Joseph had to learn that, for they did feel guilt over their cruelty to their brother. There is no sense in torturing ourselves with regrets over what might have been or with remorse over our sins. Rather, we need to turn these emotions over to God. For God alone can help us forget what we need to forget.

PRAYER ━━━━━━━━━━━━━━━━━━━━━━━━━━━

God of all compassion, if we could just forget the wounds of the past, it could make such a difference in our attitude today. We can't do it on our own, but you can make us forget what we need to forget.   *Amen.*

49

15

Whatsoever things are true, whatsoever things are honest, whatsoever things are just, whatsoever things are pure, whatsoever things are lovely, whatsoever things are of good report . . . think on these things.

Philippians 4:8 (KJV)

READ FOR REFLECTION

Reminiscing can be compared to the act of polishing pearls that have been stored away. We cultivate new pearls as we go through life, and we add them to our necklace of experiences. As we reminisce, we polish the pearls that we have cultivated through living and have stored away in the attics of our minds. Through reflection, over and over again, we remind ourselves that we have lived in the world and, in a small or great way, have made a difference. The feeling of accomplishment achieved when reminiscing allows us to have a sense of personal history. Remembering makes this possible. It is crucial, therefore, to be permitted to remember the recent and the distant past to enable us to finalize our life history.

ODACIR H. OLIVEIRA

MEDITATION

Holding On to Memories

Most people have played the parlor game of naming two or three things they would take with them if their home were threatened by fire. It is fascinating how many people will name items that preserve family history and old memories—photograph albums; objects that stir memories of trips taken. We rightly treasure our roots, for our family stories help us remember who we are.

There is a vast difference between people, on the one hand, being stuck in ihe past and, on the other, creatively remembering their history. Moses, speaking for the Lord, told the children of Israel to "remember" as they entered the promised land. Memory of God's gracious acts in their history was crucial as they entered a new world.

Yes, we need to forget old resentments and bitterness. But we need to remember those experiences of our past which remind us how we have lived in this world, which help define our existence. God's grace can allow us to look back over our lives and to affirm "It was better than I thought!"

PRAYER

Help us, Lord, to remember the joy and forget the pain. *Amen.*

16

 Therefore do not worry about tomorrow, for tomorrow will worry about itself. Each day has enough trouble of its own.

Matthew 6:34 (NIV)

READ FOR REFLECTION

To live a day at a time means, quite obviously, to stop living in the past. And how many of us do it! We have never learned how to forget "those things which are behind." It is such a temptation for us to use up our powers living over the past, and regretting old mistakes, shortcomings, and decisions, and when we do, we have so little strength left to grapple with the insistent problems and tasks immediately before us. . . . After all, God promises strength and wisdom and endurance only for today. [God] promises grace for each contest as it comes; never for the entire season's schedule. "As thy days, so shall thy strength be." Not as thy weeks, or months, or seasons, or years, but as thy DAYS. Each day we are given spiritual manna sufficient for that particular day's needs. Nothing more, and nothing less. Jesus tells us that we are to pray each day only for what is needed in that twenty-four-hour period. "Give us *this day* our daily bread." To ask for anything more is to ask for what God has not promised.

WILLIAM B. ELLIOT, JR.

MEDITATION

Ironing with the Hottest Iron

Some of us remember the old days when our mothers used flatirons to press clothes. They would line them up on the fireplace and choose the hottest iron to get the job done. Even in our later years, we may have too many irons in the fire. Perhaps our lives have gotten overcrowded, like suitcases packed beyond their limits.

We have more free time, but it seems that more demands are placed on us and we can volunteer ourselves to exhaustion. We may find ourselves pulled and stretched by a thousand and one good things, until we reach our breaking point.

Jesus said, "Do not worry about tomorrow. . . . Each day has enouch trouble of its own" (Matt. 6:34, NIV). Strike with the hottest iron. One thing at a time.

Jesus told the distracted Martha, "Martha, Martha, you are anxious and troubled about many things; one thing is needful" (Luke 10:41-42, RSV). Life is to be lived from a divine center. Here a life of amazing peace and power is available.

PRAYER ━━━━━━━━━━━━━━━━━━━━━━━━━━━━━

Gracious God, help us this day to concentrate on the things at hand and to focus on what you would have us do. Remind us that only as we are centered on you will we be delivered from distractions. *Amen.*

"For I know the plans I have for you," declares the Lord, "plans to prosper you and not to harm you, plans to give you hope and a future."

Jeremiah 29:11 (NIV)

READ FOR REFLECTION

A PLACE OF MY OWN

I like tidying up this place, Lord,
Sweeping up, wiping the sink,
Making the faucets shine.
It's not all that grand of a place, Lord,
But thank the Lord, it's mine.
It upsets my children to see me here.
"You don't have to live like this, Pop.
Live with one of us," they say.
"There's room. We'd love to have you."
What can I say?
I sound stubborn, ungrateful,
But I don't want to leave this place.
I'm lonely, sure. But there's nothing they can do
    about that.
Now that Margaret's gone and they're all grown.
Having a place of my own,
Snug as a ship's cabin, helps.
It's comforting. And You'll be here with me, Lord,
If, as they keep saying, "something happens."
What do they mean "if"? When.

ELISE MACLAY

MEDITATION

Creating Your Own Space

People are often defined by how and where they live. Many people cling to their homes because home may be the last bastion of security in this world. To hold on to home means to hold on to selfhood. It is good when we can stay in our homes as we grow older, but the time may come when we are unable to manage the maintenance of a house.

Like those ancient Jews, stranded as aliens in the strange, foreign land called Babylon, we may be forced to create a new space in a new place. For some it may be an apartment in a retirement community, or a room in a relative's home, or a room in a nursing home.

We can make any place "home" if we try. A favorite chair, a treasured photograph, an old radio, or pictures worn from age can give a touch of "home" to the strangest of surroundings.

It is not easy to give up our homes. But, even in that situation we *can* "sing the Lord's song in a foreign land" (Psalm 137:4, RSV). We do so by our faith and by trusting Christ, who on earth had "nowhere to lay his head" (Matt. 8:20, NIV).

PRAYER

Caring Father, help me sing the Lord's song in whatever situation I find myself today. Thank you for the gift of this day, and help me make this day count. Give me courage to assert my needs when changes have to be made. *Amen.*

18

 There is great gain in godliness with contentment; for we brought nothing into the world, and we cannot take anything out of the world.

1 Timothy 6:6-7 (RSV)

READ FOR REFLECTION

In *Naming the Whirlwind* Langdon Gilkey says that one of the joys of old age is the inner freedom no longer to expect too much of life. This freedom does not negate a sense of caring. Rather, it encompasses those things we learn in maturity; such learning seldom involves information and skills. We learn not to use up energy in anxiety. We learn to live with things we cannot change. We learn that most people are neither for us nor against us but rather thinking about other matters. We learn that no matter how much we try to please, some people are never going to like us, a notion that troubles at first but is eventually quite a relief. In other words, inner freedom comes from acknowledging the limitations of life.

KATHLEEN R. FISCHER

MEDITATION

Not Expecting Too Much

I chuckled as two dear ladies in a nursing home argued over everything. They squabbled over their ages, their grandchildren, and—it seemed—everything under the sun. But one thing they did agree on—they had learned not to expect too much from life.

When we were young, we had our dreams. We were like little children playing at the seashore, piling our sand castles toward the sky. We wanted so much out of life; we expected the moon. But as we grow older, we learn not to expect too much.

Paul says there is "great gain in godliness with contentment" (1 Tim. 6:6, RSV). He did not mean we fold our hands and resign ourselves to life. Rather, he speaks of an attitude of mind that helps us accept what cannot be changed and realize that life does have its limits.

There is wisdom in words from the hymn "My God, I Thank Thee":

> I thank thee, Lord, that thou hast kept
>   The best in store;
> We have enough, yet not too much,
>   To long for more;
> A yearning for a deeper peace
>   Not known before.

PRAYER

Giver of peace, we work every day at trying to practice the words of Paul, "I have learned, in whatever state I am, to be content" (Phil. 4:11, RSV). Help us this day. *Amen.*

19

 Be very careful, then, how you live—not as unwise but as wise, making the most of every opportunity, because the days are evil.

Ephesians 5:15-16 (NIV)

READ FOR REFLECTION

Those over sixty-five do not have the desire to kill time the way children do. It no longer drags by; it flies. It is the most precious of their possessions, and its supply is continually eroding. One person expressed it this way:

> The trouble with retirement
> I'll tell you in a rhyme
> Is, when you take a coffee break,
> You're wasting your own time.

They need time to dream, time to play, time to work, time to imagine, time to celebrate, time to serve, and time to understand.

BLAINE TAYLOR

MEDITATION

Balancing This Free Time

People soon learn that the free time they have when they retire can be a "mixed bag." On the one hand, not punching a time clock or living by the calendar can be liberating. But sometimes more demands await us. One retired woman, overloaded with volunteer work, said, "I work harder now than when I was employed, and I don't even get paid for it."

Anna and Simeon, two of God's older saints, balanced their time. They served God in the temple, but they always took time for reflection and prayer as they awaited the Messiah's arrival. When Mary and Joseph brought the young Jesus into the temple, Anna and Simeon were spiritually prepared to recognize him.

They both had spent much time in prayer and fasting, and it was more than luck that they were present in the temple when the young Christ Child came. When they recognized Jesus as the promised Messiah, they were quick to witness, to tell the news to all who looked forward to the deliverance promised by God.

One reason I have problems with all the furor over mandatory retirement is that it overlooks our need to do nothing. Yes, we want to be active, but we need time for renewal and reflection. Jesus knew how to find this creative balance between work and rest. Older people need this spiritual direction also; so, along with the words of "Dear Lord and Father of Mankind," we pray, "Take from our souls the strain and stress, and let our ordered lives confess the beauty of thy peace."

PRAYER

Source of all being, help us to find that creative balance between being active and being quiet. *Amen.*

Who is left among you that saw this house in its former glory? How do you see it now? Is it not in your sight as nothing?

Haggai 2:3 (RSV)

READ FOR REFLECTION

The fault of age is that it has come to a stage when it prefers things as they are. Age is a little tired; and age is a little disillusioned. It is sadly true that the only lesson that a great many people have drawn from life is that there are a large number of things which can't be done, and which are not worth trying.

WILLIAM BARCLAY

MEDITATION

Avoiding Old-Age Temptations

Those who survived the Exile and returned to Jerusalem held fast to the old temple. They refused to believe that another temple could be built that would in any way equal the former glory of Solomon's temple. Some work had been accomplished, but the elders shook their heads in contempt.

One major temptation of older people is to get stuck in the past and not be open-minded to new things. We prefer things as they were. Instead of "standing on the promises, we sometimes prefer to sit on our premises."

Sometimes we feel the nostalgia for days gone past, days that were filled with good things that will never be again. But life needs to be lived in the "now." Joy can be found now, in the beauties of God's world, an evening spent with friends and family, or quiet moments of reflection.

Jesus was always "going further." His enemies tried to trap him in the grave, but he burst from the rock-ribbed past into the new day of resurrection morning. Even as older people we can sing,

Christ of the upward way, My Guide divine,
Where Thou hast set Thy feet May I place mine,
And move and march wherever Thou hast trod,
Keeping face forward up the hill of God.

PRAYER

Sovereign God, may we never be so old as to cling to outmoded habits or get stuck in our ways. *Amen.*

And your young men shall see visions,
and your old men shall dream dreams:
yea, and on my menservants and my
   maidservants in those days
I will pour out my Spirit; and they shall
   prophesy.

Acts 2:17-18 (RSV)

READ FOR REFLECTION

The first part of life is the time to grow in the use of "head, hands, and heart," to grow "in wisdom, grace, and age." While these are lifelong activities, they are the primary task of the First Age.

The Second Age is marked by autonomy and certain fundamental choices; what I am to value and cherish, what persons and causes I am to identify with, what I am to do as work, who my friends are to be, whether I am to marry and have children, where I am to live. . . .

For all too many, descent into one's "declining years" is the signal for a kind of inertia to set in, a lapse of energy and purpose that precludes a creative approach to the rest of life. But the Third Age, whether viewed within a secular or sacred context, can be a time of conscious decision making, a graceful period in which older persons may return the gifts they have received, a time to reengage with the broader society, not alone as a family member and as a worker but as a citizen of the world with the heavy responsibility to give.

CHARLES J. FAHEY

MEDITATION

Affirming Our Third Age

Aging is a journey. We begin to age the moment we are born. During the first age, life revolves around family and school. It is the age of preparation, of getting ready for responsible adulthood.

In the second age, we find our place in the world and settle down. We establish our families and we get used to our role in the world of work. Then comes the third leg of the journey, when we are no longer as concerned with achievement or with primary care of our children. What then? Is it "out to pasture" time?

No, this is the time for new directions on our life's journey. We are wiser, more experienced, and calmer than ever before. We can continue to grow and expand our horizons as we grow, develop, and live a meaningful third age.

Are the words of Robert Browning "Grow old along with me, the best is yet to be" really true? Or do our aging bodies mock us and restrict our growth? If we see growing older as a new leg on life's journey, *a third age* of life, we might be surprised by the good that God has in store for us.

> And in that light of life I'll walk
> Till traveling days are done.
> (from "I Heard the Voice of Jesus Say")

PRAYER

God of all generations, we have lived through the first two ages—and made it so far. Help us now to make our Third Age the best years of our lives.   *Amen.*

Old Age Vulnerabilities

The aches and pains of old age and, alas, the sufferings, long or short, that so often precede death
are neither easy to see nor to endure. Even with
modern medication pain is sometimes intense and
seemingly unbearable in-between times. And then
there is the quiet suffering of the old and bedridden
ones who have lost the human dignity of taking care of
their personal and basic needs. These people seem to have
a right to ask: "Is this what life comes to?"

Eugene S. Geissler

22

Read 2 Samuel 19:31-40

 But Barzillai said to the king, ". . . I am now eighty years old; can I discern what is pleasant and what is not? Can your servant taste what he eats or what he drinks? Can I still listen to the voice of singing men and singing women? Why then should your servant be an added burden to my lord the king?"

2 Samuel 19:35 (RSV)

READ FOR REFLECTION

It is never easy to take on another person's burden, even when things are going smoothly, but there are some periods in life when it's almost impossible. Ironically enough, it very often happens that older people begin to need more support just at the point when their children's lives are the most complicated and their responsibilities are the heaviest. . . .

If, in establishing their life's priorities, sons and daughters have not been able to assign first—or even second or third—place to their parents, they may never forgive themselves. But if they try to shoulder their parents' burdens as well as their own, they may feel continually resentful and put-upon, wondering as the days go by, "When is there going to be enough time for me?" No matter which course they decide to take, they are likely to carry an additional burden: guilt.

BARBARA SILVERSTONE and HELEN KANDEL HYMAN

MEDITATION

We Don't Want to Be a Burden

Barzillai tactfully refused King David's offer to care for him in the royal court at Jerusalem as repayment for helping David and his men when David was fleeing from Absalom. Barzillai was realistic about his advanced age and did not want to be a burden to the king. He decided to return to his familiar, haunts and to spend his latter years in Gilead.

Aging parents often say they do not want to be a burden to their families. Maintaining our independence is one of the final dignities that exists for older people. Maggie Kuhn is right when she argues that we ought to place a moratorium on building too many nursing homes and to help older people stay in their own homes. Perhaps congregate housing is part of the answer.

Paul did tell us to "bear one another's burdens, and so fulfill the law of Christ" (Gal. 6:2, RSV). This does not mean that we bear burdens *for* others, but bear burdens *with* others, since every person will have to bear his or her own load (see Gal. 6:5).

David seemed to respect Barzillai's request and did not try to dissuade him from returning to his own home. Is there not a hint of kindness here as David affirmed the right to independence of his aged colleague? Whenever possible, adult children need to honor the independence of their aging parents.

PRAYER ━━━━━━━━━━━━━━━━━━━━━━━━━━━━

Strength of the weak, I don't want to be a burden to my family. Their lives are so crowded and complicated now; I don't want to add their worries. Give me strength to manage my own life, and when I can no longer be in control, let me make other plans. *Amen.*

23

Read 2 Corinthians 12:1-10

The Lord said to me, "My grace is sufficient for you, for my power is made perfect in weakness." Therefore I will boast all the more gladly about my weaknesses, so that Christ's power may rest on me.

2 Corinthians 12:9 (NIV)

READ FOR REFLECTION

Today's news is frightening. International tensions of every kind threaten peace and equilibrium. I read about a future in which the trust funds of Social Security may be exhausted, about a world in which the building of schools must give way to the building of housing for increasing numbers of the elderly, most of whom may be women.

I realize that I, too, am growing old.

I wonder if my children will have to become parents to me. They have no such obligation, of course. Nevertheless, I want them to know some of my wishes for my own latter days. I do not wish heroic measures to be used to extend my life if it has become a mere existence. They should understand my wishes regarding the time of my death, and how I feel about disability if that should intervene.

I must begin to do some things for myself, looking ahead not only to retirement but also to my own death.

JOHN GILLIES

MEDITATION

We Are Vulnerable

"I don't like being so vulnerable," said the elderly gentleman as he stared at me through those crystal blue eyes. He sat in a wheelchair, strapped in for his own protection. "I'm sick and tired of depending on others," he continued. I ached for him.

As I watched the nurse bring him his hourly tranquilizer, I thought, *How vulnerable and helpless he is.* Yet, isn't there a touch of Christ in being vulnerable? Only as Christ was vulnerable and suffered does he really break through to us. Christ's weakness on the cross becomes the place of our redemption.

The weaknesses and wounds of older people may be the very place of healing and power. If nothing else, letting others care for us may be a gift to them. Our weakness can be a bridge to relationships; our wounds the place of healing for others.

PRAYER

Sustaining Lord, we do feel so helpless at times, and we hate to rely on others. So many of us are of independent stock. Give us grace to realize our strength.   *Amen.*

Behold, I am doing a new thing;
   now it springs forth, do you not perceive it?
I will make a way in the wilderness
   and rivers in the desert.

Isaiah 43:19 (RSV)

READ FOR REFLECTION

In their declining years, most men and women relish dreaming their lonely dreams of a nostalgically remembered past. One of the great temptations of old age is to escape from an unfriendly present and an unpromising future into the pleasant memories of the past. . . .

Returning to memories of their past, many aging people show a preference for their early life, the period of childhood and youth. Gradually, an idealized version of their past life emerges in the imagination and soon also in their conversation. "When I was young, we didn't behave like that. . . . People were really friendly then. . . . " As the community pays less attention to them and their self-esteem is slipping, many aging men are tempted to bolster up their own image of the past by exaggerating their accomplishments and glorifying their past greatness and importance.

ALFONS DEEKEN

MEDITATION

Old-Age Dropouts

Jesus knew it was impossible to put the new wine of the gospel into the old wineskins of tradition. So he chose disciples from the common people, men of the sand and soil who would respond to the new truth he taught about. Those Pharisees acted like "old-age dropouts," fixated on their traditions.

As older adults we need to beware of becoming like them. We have heard of dropouts from school, but old-age dropouts are those who drop out of life's vibrancy. They become preoccupied with the past when, they insist, everything was so much better. Like school dropouts, they never get beyond a certain grade level.

Growth demands change. To live is to change. The opposite of change is rigidity, but to be alive is to be flexible. Growth is never the simple addition of something new to what is already present. To add to what is means changing the old in some way.

Isaiah saw "a new thing" springing forth in the history of Israel. It was a new exodus and a new beginning for God's people. Real growth is letting go without knowing in advance what will happen. That takes faith. But isn't the risk worth it? Isn't this better than being old-age dropouts?

PRAYER

Help me, O God, to be open to myself and to your life-giving spirit. Then I can be open to others and open to change and to growth. *Amen.*

25

Read Romans 5:1-5

 No, in all these things we are more than conquerors through him who loved us.

Romans 8:37 (NIV)

READ FOR REFLECTION

Yet, there are some people, rare people, who seem to suffer well, who seem to rebound from one loss after another. They do not have fewer troubles than the rest of us. No, they have their share of sufferings, maybe even more than most, but they still seem to appreciate life and look forward to living. They seem to have a deep acceptance of life or faith in life's goodness that sustains them and carries them through all of life's sorrows. . . .

All this is made possible, in part, because of their faith. Through faith, their losses have been transformed into transitions, new life has emerged out of old, resurrection has followed death. Thus these rare people now come to the end of their lives with a measure of assurance that the same God who brought them through all of life's previous losses will also walk with them through this final loss, together into the world beyond.

R. SCOTT SULLENDER

MEDITATION

We Triumph over Our Troubles

Bill had a wonderful sense of humor and a contagious enthusiasm for life. I can still see him sitting in that nursing home, wearing the faded cowboy hat he loved so well. He had suffered more than his share of losses in later life. First his wife, then his home, and finally his health. But his spirit was undaunted.

Once he told me that he wanted to buy a motorized cart so that he could "get around with these old folks better," but that never happened. His last mode of transportation was his wheelchair. He had little of this world's goods left, only his Bible, some tattered pictures from his past, and that old cowboy hat. The nurses told me that he kept them laughing with his jokes and boisterous ways. One nurse told me that he reminded her of Zorba the Greek with his lust for life.

Bill loved the Wild West and dreamed of being a cowboy. He told me the words to one of his favorite western songs were "Don't call him a cowboy until you see how he rides." And he would add, "Don't call anyone Christian until you see how they live." The last time I saw Bill he was fantasizing about getting up a posse to corral some horse thieves. Shortly thereafter he died from a stroke.

We buried Bill's cowboy hat with him. You could call him "Christian" by the way he had lived and triumphed over his troubles.

PRAYER ━━━━━━━━━━━━━━━━━━━━━━━━━

Gracious God, help us realize that suffering produces endurance, that endurance produces character, that character produces hope, and that this is our calling as Christians. *Amen.*

26

Why are you cast down, O my soul,
 and why are you disquieted within me?
Hope in God; for I shall again praise him,
 my help and my God.

Psalm 42:5 (RSV)

READ FOR REFLECTION

You can feel better by improving what you feel.

Depression is a good example. It is said to be the most prevalent mental-health disorder for people over sixty-five. If your depression is due to physical illness, you must get treatment for that illness, but you may also feel depressed, as we have seen, simply because you can no longer do many of the things you have enjoyed. Perhaps you have liked talking to people but now there is no one to talk to. Perhaps you have enjoyed the countryside but are now cooped up in the city. Finding someone to talk to or some way of getting to the countryside will be better than remaining alone in the city taking Valium.

B. F. SKINNER and M. E. VAUGHAN

MEDITATION

Old-Age Depression

Everyone was clapping and singing that day in the nursing home. Everyone except George. He seemed so depressed. I always ask him the time, because he was a railroad man, and he loved to pull out his railroad watch and tell me the time. Today, he just sat and stared.

Some older people have reason to get depressed. Loss of health, confinement, little to do, the endless monotony of time—all can lead to depression. Sometimes it seems like a daily battle to get out of those low moods that come so often.

There is no quick fix for old-age depression. Platitudes don't help. You cannot tell older persons to "take three pills and call me in the morning," nor can you advise them to "pack up your troubles in an old kit bag, and smile, smile, smile."

It helps to remember that Jesus got depressed and troubled. Remember his anguish in Gethsemane? We all get depressed at times. But we need to find someone who will let us talk things out and then we need to rely on God's grace.

"Hope in God," said the psalmist. He was right.

PRAYER ━━━━━━━━━━━━━━━━━━━━━━━━━━━

Merciful Lord, it seems that I am having more downs than ups these days, and that bothers me. When I am depressed, give me patience that I may not succumb to feeling that life is hopeless and I am helpless. But I need to talk things over with someone, so I pray for you to guide me to that person. *Amen.*

27

 For this people's heart has grown dull, and their ears are heavy of hearing, and their eyes they have closed.

Matthew 13:15 (RSV)

READ FOR REFLECTION

Others accept the challenge and begin to turn inward, seeking the rewards of reflection, insight, accumulation of meaning and acquisition of higher consciousness about themselves, others and this world. This is when the spiritual dimensions of aging may begin to appear. . . .

There is an inner as well as outer seeing. Blind people claim that they experience an inner light that gives them both sight and hearing and they can often see more profoundly than those of us whose eyes are dependent upon outer light. With outer light and sight we may see only the surface of things. We who have eyes may have to close them in order that we may see more deeply and penetratingly by inner light. But if we can learn to see by both inner and outer light, to reflect studiously, we will be able to move nearer to the truth implicit in our experiences.

REUEL L. HOWE

MEDITATION

Presbyopia and Presbycusis

Presbyopia and *presbycusis* are two well-known words in geriatrics. They refer to the loss of sight (presbyopia), and the loss of hearing (presbycusis). Presbyopia occurs when older people get far-sighted, and the lenses of their eyes lose their elasticity. Presbycusis brings various levels of hearing loss.

According to Jesus there is a worse kind of presbyopia and presbycusis than what happens to older people. He talked about people having ears, and yet not hearing; of having capacity for sight, and yet not seeing. He saw many people blinded by prejudice, deafened by ancient traditions, too lazy to think.

In my first parish, I was called to the bedside of a member of the church who was near death. He said to me, "Preacher, I have a confession to make. I attended church all my life but never heard a word you said." "I didn't realize you were deaf," I replied. "I'm not. I was always thinking about my business."

We can keep the "eyes" and "ears" of our souls as young as ever. I once saw the following words on the bulletin board of Carolina Village Retirement Center in Hendersonville, North Carolina:

> With old age creeping up on me, to all its
>   troubles I'm resigned.
> My joints may be stiff,
>   but I will not have rheumatism of the mind.

That's the spirit!

PRAYER ━━━━━━━━━━━━━━━━━━━━━━

Lord, give me "eyes of the heart" to see whom I can help this day and "ears of the soul" to hear someone's cry. Most of all, grant me the inner light which you alone can give. *Amen.*

28

 Then he said to Thomas, "Put your finger here, and see my hands; and put out your hand, and place it in my side; do not become faithless, but believing."

John 20:27 (RSV)

READ FOR REFLECTION

What is important, however, is that we make the quality of life—in whatever number of years are left to us—count in some way. May I say, the challenge is even to make the bad days count! . . .

. . . Let the marks of old age be honorable scars. Altogether barren is the cosmetic attempt to cover wrinkles in the skin. That is not the problem, despite what the cultural brainwash says.

DOUGLAS G. McKENZIE

MEDITATION

Old Scars

We all have our scars. Some of them are in our bodies, from old accidents or surgeries. They remind us of the pain we have experienced in our life's journey. Others are in our minds and hearts, from the hurt and disappointments life has handed us. Scars are road maps that tell the story of our lives. Whether physical or emotional, open or hidden, they are markers for the events of our lives. Scars are honorable marks.

The scars on his palms and in his side identified Jesus. When Thomas saw the scars of Jesus, Thomas believed. He knew this was Jesus risen from the grave. We rejoice that we have no unscarred Christ.

We older people have scars that identify us. They tell our story. A little boy once said, "Scars are what you have left after you get well." What are your scars? What are the honorable marks of your experience?

Paul could say, "I bear in my body the marks of the Lord Jesus" (Gal. 6:17, NKJV). He had so identified his life with Christ that he bore his scars. What do the scars we carry today say about us? Do any of our scars reveal that we have followed Christ?

PRAYER

Thank you, Helper of the weak, for our scars. They tell our story. May we realize they reveal who we are and what life has brought us. May we rejoice in them. *Amen.*

29

 We are afflicted in every way, but not crushed;
perplexed, but not driven to despair;
persecuted, but not forsaken; struck down,
but not destroyed.

2 Corinthians 4:8-9 (RSV)

READ FOR REFLECTION

It's not, as the saying goes, for sissies. There are some lucky ones who little by little slow down to be sure but otherwise go on to the end pretty much as usual. For the majority, however, it's like living in a house that's in increasing need of repairs. . . . The odd thing is that the person living in the house may feel, humanly speaking, much as always. The eighty-year-old body can be in precarious shape yet the spirit within as full of beans as ever. If that leads senior citizens to think of all the things they'd still love to do but can't anymore, it only makes things worse. But it needn't work that way. . . .

Eight year olds like eighty year olds have lots of things they'd love to do but can't because their bodies aren't up to it, so they learn to *play* instead. Eighty year olds might do well to take notice.

FREDERICK BUECHNER

MEDITATION

Knocked Down,
But Not Knocked Out!

Have you ever seen a boxer get knocked down, and yet with courage get off the canvas and stay in the fight? Knocked down, but not knocked out. Life is hard, and there are times when we will get knocked down.

Most aging persons have chronic health problems that do not respond to treatment as fast as those of the young. We feel knocked down. Fifty was nifty; but sixty is slowing us down, and who knows what is ahead?

Paul claims we can be "more than conquerors" (Rom. 8:37, RSV). He survived all manner of troubles, including a "thorn in the flesh" to fight the Christian battles. Nietzsche was right: "What does not kill me makes me stronger." We may be temporarily afflicted, but we can get off the canvas to fight again.

PRAYER ━━━━━━━━━━━━━━━━━━━━━━━━

Thank you, Lord, for those moments in life when we were troubled and knocked down by problems. As we have survived and have grown through these moments, you have built iron into our souls. *Amen.*

81

Even to your old age and gray hairs,
I am he, I am he who will sustain you.
I have made you and I will carry you;
I will sustain you and I will rescue you.

Isaiah 46:4 (NIV)

READ FOR REFLECTION

We older people need each other. We understand as no one younger really can what it means for your body to fail you by degrees as days and years go by. Sometimes it fails you suddenly. You're never quite ready.

All my life until I was in my eighties I thought of growing old as a gradual process that would bring a slow yielding to the inevitable. I thought I would develop a sense of peace, relief from work, and most responsibility. I envisioned myself sitting on the porch and rocking, doing just what came naturally as nature had her way with me. However, aging does not happen that way. First, depletion takes a sudden dip, then we remain on a kind of plateau for a short or even a long period, then another dip. As for peace, there is no peace or relief when it comes to feeling. The pain of love becomes more intense, along with the joy.

RUTH HOWARD GRAY

MEDITATION
Who Catches Us When We Fall?

One of the greatest fears older people have is the fear of falling. One slip or fall can mean a broken hip and a long recuperation. The deeper fear, however, is worrying whether anyone will be there to catch us when we fall and concern about not being able to take care of ourselves.

If we are fortunate, we can lean on a husband or wife, or a friend who will be there to make sure we don't fall. Or we may have to enter a nursing home and learn to depend on nurses and aides.

But the comforting thought is that we can always depend on God. Hosea gives us a touching picture of the Lord God teaching Ephraim to walk, just as a parent teaches his or her child (Hos. 11:3-4). Ephraim, like any little child, stumbles and falls, but God picks him up. So God carries us when we age, and we can lean on God's grace for daily strength.

When I visit an older person in a nursing home or one confined at home, I like to share the inspired words of Moses:

> The eternal God is your dwelling place,
>   and underneath are the everlasting arms.
> —Deut. 33:27, RSV

Those arms are the best support for all people—no matter what their age.

PRAYER ━━━━━━━━━━━━━━━━━━━━━━━━━━━━

Loving Lord, we are feeble at times, but we do have friends and family who help us. May we cherish their help, and may we never forget that you carry us when we cannot carry ourselves. *Amen.*

About midnight Paul and Silas were praying and singing hymns to God, and the prisoners were listening to them.

Acts 16:25 (RSV)

READ FOR REFLECTION

Life's front door and back door and even the side door may be locked, but you can always open a window.

Home-based need not mean home-bound. Your body may not be able to travel, but your mind, like Superman, can leap over walls in a single bounce, and your heart can wander all over the world.

Even if you can't get out of the house, if you have no car or someone to drive you, or if you're in a retirement or nursing home, don't shift gears into reverse and back away from all the fun, excitement, adventure, and independence that are waiting for you.

MARY KIMBROUGH

MEDITATION

Shut In, But Not Shut Out

Here are Paul and Silas in prison at Philippi. Yet at midnight they are praying and singing hymns to God, so that the prisoners were listening to them. They were confined, yet not controlled; they were shut in behind walls; and yet, their faith sang at midnight.

Many older people cannot get out of their homes. But, like these ancient missionaries, they can "sing at midnight." I know of one dear lady confined at home who writes letters to every member of the church and cheers them with her words of encouragement and comfort. Lines from the old poem by Frederick Langbridge ring true:

> Two men look out through the same bars:
> One sees the mud, and one the stars.

You may be confined at home, but your faith and radiant spirit can be an inspiration to those who visit you. And you may use this time as an opportunity to praise God and sing—even at midnight.

PRAYER

God of many deliverances, help us never to have closed-in souls. We may be confined, but we can still be in control of our attitudes. We may be homebound, but we can still explore. *Amen.*

32

 There is a season for everything, . . .
A time for giving birth,
a time for dying . . .
A time for tears,
a time for laughter;
a time for mourning,
a time for dancing.

Ecclesiastes 3:1, 2, 4 (JB)

READ FOR REFLECTION

Goodbyes are a part of every single day. Sometimes we choose them, and sometimes they choose us. Usually they are small, not so significant losses that do not pain us very much, but at times they are deep, powerful, wounding experiences that trail around our hearts and pain inside of us for years. . . .

. . . Goodbyes are any of those times when we find ourselves with a someone or something that has given our life meaning and value, when a dimension of our life seems to be out of place or unfulfilled. Goodbyes are all of those experiences that leave us with a hollow feeling someplace deep inside.

JOYCE RUPP

MEDITATION

The Relationship Heals

It was quite a meeting. We had just returned from visiting Bill's wife in a nursing home. Since Bill was confined to his home, totally dependent on others for transportation, he asked if I would take him by Tom's house. They had been friends for over sixty years but had not seen each other in some time.

Bill and Tom sat together for over an hour, engrossed in their renewed friendship. Tom's wife and I sat nearby, chatting quietly, captivated by the way these two veterans of the years shared their stories. They recalled earlier days, memories of their life together in the community. At times I felt like an intruder into their intimacy.

When they hugged goodbye, Tom said softly, "Thanks for coming to see me, Bill. Not many come anymore now that I am stuck at home." Bill cracked some ancient joke, and we left. They never saw each other again. But for one, brief shining moment, they were restored to former days, carefree and happy. They could not turn back the clock of the years, but they still were young in soul. The relationship does provide healing. And when this happens, it is Easter once again.

PRAYER

O God, our Companion, help us to be there for older people who are confined at home. And may we never forget the need to renew old friendships. Through Christ. *Amen.*

87

No Use Denying It

We brood about death most when we have nothing else to do. We brood much less when watching an exciting television program or doing something in which we are deeply interested. Everything we do to make old age more enjoyable reduces the time we spend in fearing death. The more reason we have to pay attention to life, the less we have to pay attention to death.

B. F. Skinner and M. E. Vaughan

33

 Do not cast me away when I am old;
    do not forsake me when my strength is gone.

Psalm 71:9 (NIV)

READ FOR REFLECTION

Now that I have said this much about things not so good in the aging years, and having mentioned my first experience of falling behind, it is only a step further to talk about the fears of old people. Among such fears is the fear of not being able to cope, especially in unfamiliar situations. Maybe this accounts for not liking to be away from home, or having to deal, even at home, with new problems or possibilities that seem to threaten personal security. When someone asks me, "How are you doing?" I often say, "I'm surviving." This doesn't mean much to that person, but to me it means that I have coped with life for another day or another week. Some of the worst times are worrying about something that never happens. It is not easy to cope with such worries and never helpful to be told not to worry. The problem is subjective, on the inside, and the solution must come from within. Even if the time passes and it *didn't* happen, the worry remains that the enemy, whoever, will be back.

EUGENE S. GEISSLER

90

MEDITATION

Not Needed Anymore

She seemed disoriented when I spoke with her as she wandered around the halls of the nursing home. Her name was Mary, a long-time resident. I asked, "How long since someone has visited you?" She replied, "Not since the 52nd of February." Her social worker confirmed it had been a long time since anyone had come to see her.

Many older people feel abandoned and useless when life moves to its end. Nothing hurts more than feeling we are no longer needed or loved. Maggie Kuhn calls it "The Detroit Syndrome," casting off the old model for the new. Only new models or persons are desirable, marketable, lovable.

What a tragedy it is when we waste older people. We make some of them feel they are surplus or non-persons. The psalmist, probably an old person at the time, concluded his prayer by asking God:

So even to old age and gray hairs,
O God, do not forsake me,
till I proclaim thy might
to all the generations to come.
Psalm 71:18 (RSV)

You can be assured that God never forsakes or rejects older people. God had been with Mary in that nursing home since the 52nd of February and would never forsake her. But what do we do with Jesus' words, "As you did it not to *one* of the least of these, you did it not to me" (Matt. 25:45, RSV)?

PRAYER ━━━━━━━━━━━━━━━━━━━━━━━━━━━━

Gracious God, it is hard to realize I am not as useful in the same ways that I once was. Sometimes I feel life is passing me by more quickly than I thought. Show me ways that I can reach out in ministry and feel that I can make a difference in someone's life. *Amen.*

91

34

 When you were young
you put on your own belt
and walked where you liked;
but when you grow old,
you will stretch out your hands,
and somebody else will put a belt around you
and take you where you would rather not go.

John 21:18 (NJB)

READ FOR REFLECTION

I don't agree with the generalization that it is unfortu-
nate that old people are sent to nursing homes. I would
prefer such if unable to care for myself. I could feel more
at ease if my burden rests on someone whose vocation it
is to care for the infirm. It is a matter of not wanting to
stunt somebody else's life.

Mind you, I do not see retirement homes and nursing
homes as aspects of Eden. My great hope is that I will be
graced with the attitude shown by the woman in a
nursing home who wrote: "So it was rough. And sometimes it was sweet. But I have lived to be ninety-three.
And that's wonderful."

EDWARD FISCHER

MEDITATION

Where We Do Not Want to Go

I stopped and spoke to the elderly gentleman strapped in a chair. He sat in a room where the only voice was that of a television announcer. He mumbled, "How I wish I could get out of here and go back to my farm." I thought, *How fortunate I am that I was not strapped in a chair; I could put on my belt this morning and go where I liked.*

Like it or not, the day may come when we will face going into a nursing home. For many older people this is still a terrible thought. Some see a nursing home as the last stop before the cemetery.

We can take courage from the example of Peter. Jesus made it clear that the days would come when Peter too would face the cross. Part of his discipleship would involve suffering and being taken where he did not want to go. Just as God's strength had been available to Peter earlier, so God would not fail him in this crisis. He could recall the words of Jesus, "I have prayed for you, Simon, that your faith may not fail" (Luke 22:32, JB).

PRAYER ━━━━━━━━━━━━━━━━━━━━━━━━━━━━━━━

Defender of the helpless, we are weak, but you are strong. We ask that whatever life brings to us, our faith may not fail. *Amen.*

35

 How shall we sing the Lord's song in a strange land?

Psalm 137:4 (KJV)

READ FOR REFLECTION

A friend of mine said the sad part about her late-in-life accomplishments is that her parents never got to see how successful she became. I'm sure this is happening to a lot of people today who don't really develop all their capabilities fully until they've experimented with life for a while.

That we must choose, at eighteen, what road to follow—and stay on that path until the end—has by now become an antiquated idea. We take it for granted that artists mature, that writers become more seasoned; that's true of all of us. But unless we try, unless we reject the thought that it's "too late," we'll never realize our potential. . . .

Fortunately, though, attitudes are changing. The more that older people stay in the mainstream of life, the more accepting generations will be of each other. Whenever anyone wants to make a point about the accomplishments one can rack up late in life, a long list of *famous* people is mentioned. The fact is *ordinary* people do it every day, and they are the ones who'll make the greatest impact.

HELEN HAYES

MEDITATION

A Displaced Person

She knew the day would come, but that didn't make it any easier. Her whole identity seemed to be wrapped up in her home and garden. So much love and energy had been poured into those flowers and rooms that to leave these was like leaving herself in the closet. She felt devastated as she prepared to move into a small one-bedroom apartment in a retirement home.

No doubt she could identify with those ancient Hebrews who had been displaced from their homes in Jerusalem and deported to the strange land of Babylon. Surrounded by people who spoke a foreign language, separated from all that was familiar, they simply could not "sing the Lord's song in a strange land." They were ready to hang up their lyres on the willows, for life seemed to have come to a screeching halt. But they did take heart; they rebuilt their lives and began again.

It is great when older people can remain in their own homes, but the day comes for some when that is no longer possible, and the feelings of displacement and homesickness are almost too much to bear. But, like those ancient Hebrews, we *can* begin life again, even in a strange place. It is God's privilege to begin life, but it is our privilege to begin life again. Older people *can* relocate with grace, retain some mementos of their past, and build a new life somewhere else.

PRAYER ▬▬▬▬▬▬▬▬▬▬▬▬▬▬▬▬▬▬▬▬▬▬▬▬▬▬▬▬

God, help us realize that you are our true home and that wherever we live, you are there. Give us courage and grace to be comfortable wherever we may live in our later years. *Amen.*

I believe that I shall see the goodness of the Lord
in the land of the living!
Wait for the Lord;
be strong, and let your heart take courage;
yea, wait for the Lord!

Psalm 27:13-14 (RSV)

READ FOR REFLECTION

The fear of death, I'm convinced, is at the bottom of all
apprehensions. To say of any of us that we do not fear
death is a lie. To be human is to fear death. To love life is
to hope and to wish not to leave it. And all people fear
death. I think that is one of the most creative fears there
is because it bestows a value, an affection, and a gratitude for life which otherwise there would not be. That is
what the Psalm (90) means by the statement "So teach
us to number our days that we may get a heart of
wisdom." . . .

JOSEPH A. SITTLER

MEDITATION

Fears May Be Liars

All of us know that death still threatens us. Luther prayed, "And though this world with devils filled, Should threaten to undo us." But it is death that is our moral enemy. Its sting hurts; its victory wrests life from loved ones.

When we are trapped by this fear of death we cannot live abundant lives. We cling to those things that appear to give life some semblance of permanence. We do not feel free to take risks, and we find it hard to give generously without counting the cost.

Yet, Jesus taught that "unless a grain of wheat falls into the earth and dies, it remains alone; but if it dies, it bears much fruit" (John 12:24, RSV). Dying, we live. Jesus didn't want death, but when it came he accepted it as part of the givenness of his life. By dying, Christ robbed death of its power and delivered us from its terror. So, fears may be liars. Even that final fear!

PRAYER ━━━━━━━━━━━━━━━━━━━━━━━━

Lord, we are more afraid of dying than of death. Give us the faith to pray as Jesus did from the cross, "Father, into thy hands I commend my spirit," so that living or dying, we are in God's hands. *Amen.*

37

 Stand by the roads, and look,
   and ask for the ancient paths,
where the good way is; and walk in it,
   and find rest for your souls.

Jeremiah 6:16 (RSV)

READ FOR REFLECTION

In early times age also conveyed a sense of power and wisdom derived from old persons having traversed so much of life and experience that no one else had. The Elders moved beyond the struggles of ordinary life. They were treated with respect and fear . . .

JOHN-RAPHAEL STAUDE

MEDITATION

No Substitute for Experience

King Rehoboam rejected the wise counsel of his elders and sided with his young advisors. The older men wanted him to be a more compassionate king and to lighten the load on the people. They counseled the king to "be a servant to this people, and serve them" (1 Kings 12:7, NIV).

The younger advisors, who were hot after power, wanted a tougher stand. They called for scorpions instead of whips. The older advisors may have been more attuned to the spiritual history of the nation.

Forgetting his own history and the oppression of his people in Egypt, Rehoboam took the advice of the young advisors, who were ingratiating themselves to the king, and disregarded the older counselors who had served his father, Solomon. The advice of the young turned out to be folly, and following it plunged the nation into a senseless civil war.

Our society still seems to worship youth and power. Physical beauty, productivity, and speed still are dominant in our culture. But in that moment of Hebrew history described in 1 Kings, the counsel of the older advisors was unquestionably right. The Israelites needed a gentler approach.

What a wealth of wisdom and experience older people have to offer! What an untapped source of counsel and knowledge! Our nation and our church would be wise to consult older people more often. There is no substitute for experience.

PRAYER ▬▬▬▬▬▬▬▬▬▬▬▬▬▬▬▬▬▬▬▬

God of Wisdom, help us respond wisely and lovingly when others turn to us for guidance and counsel. Let us listen to our peers, for they may have a word for us which will be your word. *Amen.*

38

 There is a river whose streams make glad
    the city of God,
   . . . . .
God is in the midst of her, she
    shall not be moved;
God will help her right early.
Psalm 46:4-5 (RSV)

READ FOR REFLECTION

There are times when however much we would like to
be busily engaged doing something; however much we
feel as though there are some things we just must do,
the condition of our bodies or our minds just will not
permit us to do any of the things about which we feel we
would like to be busy.

Out of my experiences recently, I have discovered that
in periods like that I sometimes can (mark I said
"sometimes," because I cannot always occupy myself
this way) use these times of enforced inactivity to think
through some of the things which I wished I had had
time for back in the days when I was busy with many
things and said to myself, "I wish I had more time to
really think about this." Or, there will be days when all
we can do is to just sit and watch the days speed dizzily
by.

CHARLES E. S. KRAEMER

MEDITATION

The Age with Nothing to Do

All the uproar about mandatory retirement misses the point. While I do not want to deprive any older person of the opportunity to work past age sixty-five, what makes people think that there ought not to be a time for doing nothing—or doing what we choose—when we retire?

An old Taoist parable expressed it this way:

> The carpenter said to his apprentice: "Do you know why this tree is so big and so old?"
>
> The apprentice said: "No . . . Why?"
>
> Then the carpenter answered: "Because it is useless. If it were useful it would have been cut down, sawed up and used for beds and tables and chairs. But, because it is useless, it has been allowed to grow. That is why it is now so great that you can rest in its shadow."

The value of that tree was in the tree itself, not in its being productive or useful. There is value in being, as well as in doing. The word of the Lord that came to the Israelites through Moses was "Stand firm, and see the salvation of the Lord" (Exod. 14:13, RSV). In a culture that still puts a premium on "busy-ness" and seems to perceive idleness as a sin, we might teach that there can be value in doing nothing.

PRAYER

Creator God, when life slows us down and we seem to spin wheels in doing nothing, let us enjoy these moments in quiet reflection and meditation. We praise you for these moments of doing nothing whereby we keep our souls. *Amen.*

39

 For to me to live is Christ, and to die is gain. . . .
My desire is to depart and be with Christ, for
that is far better.

Philippians 1:21, 23 (RSV)

READ FOR REFLECTION

ON THE DEATH OF AN AGED FRIEND

You are not dead—Life has but set you free!
  Your years of life were like a lovely song,
  The last sweet poignant notes of which, held long,
Passed into silence while we listened, we
Who loved you listened still expectantly!
  And we about you whom you moved among
  Would feel that grief for you were surely wrong—
You have but passed beyond where we can see.

For us who knew you, dread of age is past!
You took life, tiptoe, to the very last;
  It never lost for you its lovely look;
  You kept your interest in its thrilling book;
To you Death came no conquerer; in the end—
You merely smiled to greet another friend!

ROSELLE MERCIER MONTGOMERY

MEDITATION
On the Death of an Aged Friend

She was an incredible person. Although she lived in dire poverty, her spirit and homespun humor captivated everyone. Once she told me, "I would hate to smoke the devil's pipe all my life, and then blow smoke in the Lord's face when I die!"

Her body was frail and was finally ravaged by a stroke. We hated to see the aging process take over her body. She was eventually taken to a nursing home, where she died in peace. Can there be a parallel between the process of aging and readiness for death itself? She died as she lived, peacefully, with a smile on her angelic face.

Yet we all miss her. We can share the feelings of David in his lament for his friends Saul and Jonathan:

Thy glory, O Israel, is slain
    upon thy high places!
How are the mighty fallen!
      2 Sam. 1:19, RSV

The death of an old friend hurts terribly. But we take comfort knowing that the friend is with Christ, free at last.

PRAYER ━━━━━━━━━━━━━━

For all our friends whom we have loved long since and lost a while, we thank you, dear Lord. In the communion of saints they live in our hearts. *Amen.*

40

 The king was deeply moved, and went up to the chamber over the gate, and wept; and as he went, he said, "O my son, Absalom, my son, my son Absalom! Would I had died instead of you."
2 Samuel 18:33 (RSV)

READ FOR REFLECTION

Real grief is not healed by time. It is false to think that the passing of time will slowly make us forget her and take away our pain. I really want to console you in this letter, but not by suggesting that time will take away your pain, and that in one, two, three, or more years you will not miss her so much anymore. I would not only be telling a lie, I would be diminishing the importance of mother's life, underestimating the depth of your grief, and mistakenly relativizing the power of the love that has bound mother and you together for forty-seven years. If time does anything, it deepens our grief. The longer we live, the more fully we become aware of who she was for us, and the more intimately we experience what her love meant for us. Real, deep love is, as you know, very unobtrusive, seemingly easy and obvious, and so present that we take it for granted. Therefore, it is often only in retrospect—or better, in memory—that we fully realize its power and depth. Yes, indeed, love often makes itself visible in pain.

HENRI J. M. NOUWEN

MEDITATION
Acquainted with Grief

Two moments in David's life show his grief. His loss of the infant son of Bathsheba caused him sorrow and pain. But the tragic death of Absalom left scars that lasted the rest of his life. It was all so unnecessary.

Older people have a lot of grief work to do. Cherished friends die, and we feel their loss. We grieve over the loss of family members, and we grieve over our own personal losses. Society still tells us to be brave and not cry. But we know now that grieving is a helpful, healthy process. The Bible verse every Sunday school child knows by heart is the two-word verse, "Jesus wept" (John 11:35, RSV). Jesus was able to weep and express his feelings at Lazarus's death. He did not block his grief, and neither should we.

An elderly widow, whose musician husband had died twenty years before, kept his music studio as he had left it the day he died. She locked the keyboard of his piano, and no one was allowed to enter the room. Every day she stood in the doorway with her memories. Wouldn't it have been better if she had sought new friends, new directions, and opened up that keyboard?

PRACE ━━━━━━━━━━━━━━━━━━━━━

Lord, you were a "man of sorrows, acquainted with grief," so you understand our grief. We know that time does deepen our grief, but we can move beyond and forge new directions. Help us. *Amen.*

41

Precious in the sight of the Lord
is the death of his saints.
Psalm 116:15 (RSV)

READ FOR REFLECTION

Death is a subject that most people are afraid of, or that, at least, they would like to avoid. Sometimes adult children believe that the safest course is to act as if nothing has changed. If the topic of death sneaks into a conversation somehow, they quickly change the subject or say that such ideas are silly. But making death a taboo subject may prevent your parent from coming to terms with it. Dying people have a great need to talk, and to experience honest intimacy with loved ones so that the generations can mourn together, and even plan for the future. In fact, a person who knows that loved ones understand and will re–adjust is likely to have a less emotionally painful death. . . .

Some children think that if the situation's true hopelessness is expressed, a parent's will to live will plummet. Children may also avoid facing up to a parent's impending death out of fear that their feelings of hopelessness will negatively affect the quality of care they provide for their parent. Not so. Facing your parent's death means, in part, accepting the limits of your efforts without actually doing less.

JAMES HALPERN

MEDITATION
On the Death of a Parent

He called me several weeks before it happened. It was a strange call, almost a premonition of what later took place. He said that he just wanted to hear my voice and asked about the grandchildren. Several weeks later he died. His last sermon was from Micah 6:8 and dealt with finding joy in life, with making each day count.

Eleven months before his death he had gone back to Northfield, Massachusetts, where he had lived as a boy. He stood in the pulpit where Dwight L. Moody and his father had preached; it was for him a way of coming to terms with his own life and a way of saying goodbye.

Jacob made his final request to be buried in Canaan with his family—Abraham and Sarah, Isaac and Rebekah, and Leah. After Jacob's death, Joseph "fell on his father's face, and wept over him, and kissed him" (Gen. 50:1, RSV).

The death of a parent, Freud said, is one of the most traumatic experiences of life; the loss leaves a void which nothing can fill. This loss is difficult because its grief is largely ignored and under-valued. Most people think that when an older parent dies, it was expected and the son or daughter should not be upset. But we need to grieve openly for a parent's death. Even when parents attain the biblical ideal of dying "old and full of days," adult children feel baffled and bereft. One world has ended, and another has begun.

PRAYER ━━━━━━━━━━━━━━━━━━━━━━

Loving Parent, we have honored our parents on earth; we mourn their loss, but rejoice that one day we shall see their angel faces, whom we "have loved long since, and lost awhile." *Amen.*

42

No eye has seen,
  no ear has heard,
 no mind has conceived
   what God has prepared
     for those who love him.

1 Corinthians 2:9 (NIV)

READ FOR REFLECTION

"The resurrection of the body, and life everlasting. Amen." These last two things of the Creed answer most of the deepest whys about life. Actually, I am more than a little surprised about the resurrection of the body. When the body gets old, it begins to feel and look like something to be thrown away soon. But oh, how we do need our bodies! How can we function without them? How in the dim shades of tomorrow can anyone recognize us without our bodies? I am hoping my resurrection of the body will catch me at my very best moment of life, or better still, that I come up with a glorified body like Jesus did, not subject to the limitations of space and time.

EUGENE S. GEISSLER

MEDITATION

And the Life Everlasting

Many older people still shy away from talk about life beyond. A wife and her husband were making plans for retirement, and she said, "I feel that no matter which one of us dies first, after it is over, *I* will go to Florida to live with my sister."

We fill our days with busy work, and even as we grow older, often we shut out thoughts of death. But the glorious truth of Jesus' resurrection can shatter our fear of death. To deny death is to deny the resurrection. When we realize that what happened to Jesus' body will happen to ours, death seems less final.

The gates guard their secrets well, and no one really knows what the next life will be. But, as we relive through scripture and liturgy Christ's forty days between Easter and the Ascension, we catch our only glimpse. As John the beloved disciple said, "Beloved, we are God's children now; it does not yet appear what we shall be, but we know when he appears we shall be like him, for we shall see him as he is" (1 John 3:2, RSV).

Resurrection is one of the Christian beliefs that is crucial for older people. We know that resurrection is always a miracle, a gift of the God who calls forth life from death. We rejoice that beyond the depths of winter and old age, there will be yet another spring.

> O blest communion, fellowship divine!
> We feebly struggle, they in glory shine.

(from "For All the Saints")

PRAYER

God of hope and joy, help us really to believe that we shall be raised from our old bodies to a new and glorious body. Help us to walk by faith and not by sight. *Amen.*

Keeping the
Spirit Renewed

The beautiful people I have known in the latter part of the mid-life journey are beautiful people when Christ is working his ministry of renewal inside them. Always, . . . I feel that they are being what Paul calls 'inwardly renewed'. . . . by the person's openness to Christ's work within him or her.

Douglas G. McKenzie

They will still bear fruit in old age,
they will stay fresh and green.
Psalm 92:14 (NIV)

READ FOR REFLECTION

Since prayer is the main part of a relationship with God, elderly people who have known many happy relationships during their lives may need little help to grow into the most wonderful relationship of all. For many there will be a quiet natural growth and enjoyment of conversation with a friend who can be loved and trusted. We shall simply have to remember that God is always there, waiting for us, ready to pray with us and within us. We shall move naturally from thanking . . . and showing our needs, to prayer for others, and then perhaps to the prayer of silence, to wordless adoration and communion. It is the desire and the will that matter, not the methods, nor the aids, though these things can help us.

SUSAN COUPLAND

MEDITATION

Learning to Pray in Old Age

We remember that when our children left home for college or work we felt helpless and realized all we could do was pray for them. Praying for them meant that we could be with them, without being there. Isn't that a meaningful sense of prayer?

When we were younger we claimed that we prayed as we worked. Instead of saying, "Let's pray about it," we got involved. But now that we are older and life has slowed us down, reflective prayer becomes more vital. Behind the scenes we can maintain a life of prayer and inward worship. And in our hearts we can "flash a prayer" for loved ones and for God's children in the world.

We need to forget all the *talk* about prayer—and start praying! We need to be as persistent as the nagging widow in Jesus' parable in Luke 18:1-8, the widow who persisted until she was heard. Who knows? One of the most valuable ministries older people can offer may be keeping the windows of our souls open to another world.

PRAYER THOUGHT ━━━━━━━━━━━━━━

Now, as in younger days, we are like those first disciples asking Jesus, "Lord, teach us to pray" (Luke 11:1, RSV). Perhaps our prayer as older people could be, "Lord, help us to keep on praying. *Amen.*"

Jesus said, "Let her alone; why do you trouble her? She has done a beautiful thing to me. . . . She has done what she could."

Mark 14:6, 8 (RSV)

READ FOR REFLECTION

A STORY

Once there were two great organists in a cathedral town. On Sundays they took turns playing for the high mass. Both knew their music and both played so well the huge old organ seemed to speak.

Yet the two musicians played differently. People who knew little about music felt, rather than understood, the difference. Most were drawn to the older of the two organists and did not know why.

One Sunday, after an especially dazzling performance, the younger organist went to the older and said, "I heard you play today. I could have played every note you played, but somehow my music would not be like yours. Your whole soul seems to escape into the melody."

The older man smiled an embarrassed smile and replied, "You are right. My soul is in my music, but so is yours and so, too, is the soul of every person in this church who tries to sing. As you grow older and suffer more, your soul will grow also. As it does, it will fill your music with a unique beauty all your own."

WILLIAM V. COLEMAN

MEDITATION

She Did What She Could

Once active in life, she was now confined to a small apartment. She had no transportation, and she couldn't get to church unless someone remembered to bring her. She told me that she hated to depend on others, but without any family close by, she was marooned without someone's help. At times she seemed depressed about being a "comfortable prisoner" and admitted she felt sad about having so little to contribute to her church.

Yet, this eighty-year-old lady never seemed to lose her sense of humor or her love of playing the piano. On one occasion she told me, "I have four men friends. I get up with Will Power. I eat breakfast with Arthur Ritis. I go for a walk with Charley Horse. And I go to bed with Ben Gay." We laughed about that! She was always chuckling over her fading memory and her inability to get names straight.

She still played the piano, and when someone would bring her to the Senior Outreach Satellite at the church she would charm everyone with the old songs. The other seniors would gather around the piano, and "chords that were broken would vibrate once more." Once she played "A Land Where We'll Never Grow Old," and it seemed to describe her spirit. Like the woman who broke open the alabaster jar of ointment at Jesus' feet, she did what she could.

PRAYER ━━━━━━━━━━━━━━━━━━━━━━━━━━━━

Let us learn, dear Lord, that neither are we too old nor is it ever too late to do something for the kingdom. Let us remember that Jesus blessed the little things, the cup of cold water, the widow's mite, the little acts of kindness. *Amen.*

45

 For now we see in a mirror dimly, but then face to face.

1 Corinthians 13:12 (RSV)

READ FOR REFLECTION

The last time I saw Anna Freud, the distinguished child psychoanalyst and the daughter of Sigmund Freud, she was 84 years old and in declining health—though her mind was as wonderfully alert and thoughtful as ever.

"I wish I had given more reflection and study to elderly people," she told me a bit wistfully. "Toward the end of life I think certain psychological truths become especially clear—because we have less energy to hide ourselves! Many men and women who are called 'old' and 'retired' are living up to the best in themselves, and it's a pity we don't ask for their help. They have much to offer the world."

She explained to me that she regarded older people as less inclined to "pretend," to "play hide-and-seek with themselves," and thus more able to offer a "directness," a "freshness of spirit" that can be helpful to younger people caught up in the trials, the conceits and, alas, the deceits of contemporary living.

ROBERT COLES

116

MEDITATION

No Halloween Masks in a Nursing Home

It was a Halloween party at a nursing home, and most of the residents were costumed or wearing masks. One older gentleman wore a mask that actually resembled his real face. In fact, when he took off the mask, he didn't change that much. What a parable of old age! Most older people do not wear masks. They are what they are.

At that same party, one dear lady did not like the music being sung by a guest soloist. So she blurted out, "If you don't sing 'Frosty the Snow Man,' just go on home." Her honesty made us all laugh.

There is something refreshing about the honesty of most older people. They rip off their "masks" and "tell it like it is." In this world of plastic people, where we endlessly try to mirror what others want us to be, it *is* refreshing to be with older people who are what they are. With them other people can be themselves.

PRAYER ━━━━━━━━━━━━━━━━━━━━━━━━━━━━━

Merciful One, help us be real people, rejoicing in who we are, not trying to be echoes of what others expect us to be. May we celebrate our uniqueness. *Amen.*

46

 We know that all things work together for good to them that love God, to them who are called according to the will of God.

Romans 8:28 (KJV)

READ FOR REFLECTION

. . . Aging's third lesson: there have been "golden flecks amidst the ashes." This expression is from a novel in which a prince, on his deathbed, takes stock of his life.

He was making up a general balance sheet of his whole life, trying to sort out of the immense ash-heap of liabilities the golden flecks of happy moments. . . . Could those latter hours be really put down to the credit side of life? Were they not some sort of anticipatory gift of the beatitudes of death? It didn't matter, they had existed.

(Giuseppe di Lampedusa, *The Leopard*, trans. Archibald Colquhoun, [New York: Pantheon Books, 1960] 288-89). . . .

It is not, I suspect, much different for any of us as our time winds down. Few great lives come into the world, and, witness Methuselah, longevity hardly assures greatness. Fortunately age allows one to see that unrelieved greatness is not the point. The golden flecks along the way enable one to ward off the demons of despair and self-disgust. . . . Quantitatively we may all deserve condemnation, but the "golden flecks," perhaps infrequent and certainly transient, still shine.

DAVID J. MAITLAND

MEDITATION

Golden Flecks amid the Ashes

Helen Hayes once wrote about the value of experience. She said, "Older people do us an injustice if they choose not to share their experience. . . . A woman named Thelma Ruble put it like this: 'I'm not living on borrowed time. I'm living on given time.' "

Some older people resist looking back at their lives because they feel they really have not accomplished that much. One older man told our Life Review Group that he did not want to share his life story. "Who would want to hear my story?" he asked. How sad.

Most of us have looked at our past and have wondered if we would have acted differently in light of what we know now. We dream about the past, and at times we complain about the blows life has dealt us.

We might have done things differently, but I doubt it. We did the best we could under the circumstances, and somehow muddled through it. But our faith tells us that God works all things together for good. God is not a Mr. Fixit to give us happy endings, but a Presence to grant us strength to bear whatever happens.

Von Herkomer was a gifted artist, but one particular work seemed shapeless and a waste. He fell asleep, completely defeated. When he awoke, the sun's rays shone on his art, and he exclaimed, "Why, it's better than I thought!" So with our lives. There are golden flecks amid the ashes.

PRAYER

God who gives us hope, thank you again for your grace, which has sustained us all through life. We look back and often get sad about our mistakes and blunders. But your grace has turned our disappointments into your appointments. *Amen.*

119

47

 He [your grandson] will renew your life and sustain you in your old age.

Ruth 4:15 (NIV)

READ FOR REFLECTION

What restores a grandparent's soul? The very same thing that restores anyone's soul: respect and honor personally and publicly expressed. The old, because of the realities of aging, need that respect, orchestrated in society and in one's children. But perhaps there is one group that if left on their own need laws to do what has to be done. Perhaps they respect experience and authority that does not come into direct conflict with them—rather they serve as models of what one can ideally respect. Perhaps grandchildren naturally fit this bill and mean so much to their grandparents because it is these children who naturally put them on a pedestal and thereby restore their souls.

HARLAN J. WECHSLER

MEDITATION

Grandchildren Renew Our Lives

Naomi, in the Book of Ruth, suffered devastating losses in her life. First, her husband, Elimelech, died in Moab, and ten years later her sons, Mahlon and Chilion died. Now, later in life, she is comforted by the birth of a grandson, Obed. Her friends say to her, "He shall be to you a restorer of life and a nourisher of your old age" (Ruth 4:15, RSV).

On the one hand, following the biblical laws of levirate marriage (Deut. 25:5-6), the child will carry on her son's name, and perhaps it is the certainty of continuity that will renew her life. Naomi nurses her grandson (Ruth 4:16, RSV), and the women end their congratulations by saying, "A son has been born to Naomi" (Ruth 4:17, RSV). This seems a strange saying when one remembers that the son was born to Ruth, not to her mother-in-law.

But, on the other hand, there is something special about grandchildren. When Naomi held little Obed in her arms, she not only felt joy over the assured future of her family name; she must have experienced that renewal of life which comes with the birth of a child. No wonder the ancient psalmist prayed, "May you see your children's children!" (Psalm 128:6 RSV). Grandchildren are a wonder. Their antics amuse us; their presence evokes deep and mysterious feelings; they provide a spark of joy in our aging years.

PRAYER ━━━━━━━━━━━━━━━━━━━━━━━━━━━━━

For the laughter of little grandchildren, the way they brighten our days and make our later years so full of joy, we will always be grateful, dear God. *Amen.*

48

Truly I say to you, this poor widow has put in more than all those who are contributing to the treasury. . . . She out of her poverty has put in everything she had, her whole living.

Mark 12:43-44 (RSV)

READ FOR REFLECTION

The frail elderly in your congregation will call upon many of your skills. Although they are a minority of the old, they may have majority needs which can require the resources of all of us. Like the hypoactive children "who never give teachers a minute's trouble" but who may be desperately troubled themselves, these frail elderly quietly hide away in the closets of their needs.

In pockets of every town and city are the invisible old, the ones who have grown old and then poor or ill or both, who are out of sight in their homes or rooms, existing only with vestiges of pride and large quantities of aloneness. They may feel shame that they do not have the clothes for going to worship or the transportation to get there. They may be unable to contribute much money; their pride is all that is left; and they sometimes hold to it in their lonely rooms.

They won't trouble you. You may not even know they are present. Until you are called upon to perform the funeral service you may not realize that they are dying from the grave affliction of loneliness.

BERT KRUGER SMITH

MEDITATION

The Might of a Widow

Pearl lived such a simple life. Her husband had left her with only a meager Social Security allowance, and she had no other income or assets except the little house where she lived. She told me that her major worry was being able to remain in her own home, among her own furniture and the pictures of her family. Yet she never seemed to complain, but constantly spoke about the "goodness of the Lord."

One day as I visited her in that two-room house, with the blinds drawn, and that old musty smell, she handed me her church offering and told me to put it in the collection plate. "I have always tried to give my 'mite,'" she said. I felt embarassed to take any money from this needy person, but then I remembered another widow's mite.

The widow that Jesus mentioned in Mark's Gospel put in two copper coins, which equaled a penny. Yet, her gift counted for more than all the other gifts, because she gave everything. And she gave it out of love. As I slowly left Pearl's house, I felt that both the widow that Jesus recognized and Pearl had something in common. They were poor, yet rich. They were weak, yet strong. They had stored up treasures in heaven. Both were "pearls of great price" and are not forgotten by Christ.

PRAYER ━━━━━━━━━━━━━━━━━━━━━━━

Watchful and caring God, who has chosen what is weak in the world to shame the strong, we praise you for the little people whom we meet that remind us of your kingdom. Help us remember that our power is made perfect only in weakness. *Amen.*

49

They who wait for the Lord shall renew their
    strength,
  they shall mount up with wings as eagles;
they shall run and not be weary,
  they shall walk and not faint.

Isaiah 40:31 (RSV)

READ FOR REFLECTION

One of the best uses of leisure in retirement is walking. I learned quite young that walking puts me in touch with the moods of all times of day and all turns of season. As a student I knew what Søren Kierkegaard meant in admonishing: "Above all, do not lose your desire to walk. Every day I walk myself into a state of well-being, and walk away from every illness. I have walked myself into my best thoughts, and I know of no thought so burdensome that one cannot walk away from it."

While gathering material for *Why Americans Retire Abroad* I met an elderly New Yorker who explained why he had retired to the Costa del Sol in Southern Spain: "Here I can walk every day. In New York that was not possible. When you get my age you must walk *every* day!"

EDWARD FISCHER

MEDITATION

Walk to Sunrise

Walking is a priority for older people. As long as we are able, we cherish those moments when we can walk. We hate to think of the day that may come when we have to use a walker, or are an invalid. Walking is not only good exercise, but it helps clear our minds and gives us time for quiet reflection.

Psychologists tell us that brisk walks increase our feelings of energy, sometimes for several hours. Walks are far more effective for energy than a candy bar. They reduce stress and make personal problems seem less serious. Walking helps us to sort things out.

In the Hebrew scriptures we read about Enoch, who walked with God. The prophet Micah urges us to "walk humbly with your God" (Mic. 6:8, RSV). The prophet Isaiah foresaw the coming kingdom as a place where "the redeemed shall walk there" (Isa. 35:9, RSV). Walking is not only good for our bodies and minds, but it is soul food. And let us not forget that older people walk to the sunrise. As the words of the hymn "I Heard the Voice of Jesus Say" tell us:

> I looked to Jesus,
> and I found in him my star, my sun;
> And in that light of life I'll walk
> Till traveling days are done.

PRAYER

O God, help us to be grateful for small blessings, like being able to walk in your good world. Our pace may be slower, and yet our peace is greater because we take the time to commune with you. *Amen.*

125

50

 And when they had eaten their fill, he [Jesus] told his disciples, "Gather up the fragments left over, that nothing may be lost."

John 6:12 (RSV)

READ FOR REFLECTION

In our stereotyped way of seeing the elderly, we see isolation, depression and despair. We see the inexorable loss of friends and faculties, a gradual, irreversible decline. But in truth depression can strike at any age, nor are most old people depressed. And while death seems to be more a factor in our lives as we age, it is only because we do such a good job of blocking it out of our awareness while we are younger. Then there is the image of Grandma or Grandpa, . . . on the porch "contemplating." Perhaps. But there are at least as many grandpas and grandmas leading healthy, active and loving lives. We don't usually think of these people because of the unconscious power of our stereotypes.

RAYMOND J. STOVICH

MEDITATION

Fragments Can Be Valuable

A Sunday school class had been studying the lives of the twelve disciples of Jesus. Reviewing the lesson the following week, the teacher asked the children about those first friends of Jesus. She quizzed the students about what these friends were called. An awkward pause ensued, until one little girl waved her hand and said, "I know. I know. They were God's recycles."

After Jesus fed the multitudes he told the disciples to gather up the fragments. Those fragments served a future purpose. So it is with older people. Too often we feel like rejects and culls, fragments of potential. But we do not have to succumb to the attitude that people work, produce, quit, and then die. We can be affirmed for our *worth*, not just our *work*.

God never wastes people. We are valuable to God as long as we live. We need to make our remaining years count for the kingdom. Yes, we may feel like fragments, but we are still valuable in the kingdom of heaven.

PRAYER

Loving God, I suppose it is hard for me to realize that I can still be useful to you and to others. Sometimes I feel so fragmented and stretched in different directions. Then, you amaze me with some situation where my experience and wisdom still help someone else. Thank you. *Amen.*

51

Read Psalm 77

I consider the days of old,
  I remember the years long ago.
I commune with my heart in the night;
  I meditate and search my spirit.
                    Psalm 77:5-6 (RSV)

READ FOR REFLECTION

I am seventy-seven years old. Some of the last thirteen years have been the happiest of my life. I will not say, "Old age is the golden age." It's seldom that easy. But it may be a kind of gold mine since gold can be found there if we search and dig.

I also think of old age as a time when ripe plums drop less often in our laps. We have to climb the tree to get them. But climbing can be fun. It keeps us in condition. And the plums are worth it. When people ask my secret of a happy old age, I answer that it's the grace of God mediated through determination, persistence, and hard work—on myself.

SARAH–PATTON BOYLE

MEDITATION

Our Disappointments, God's Appointments

I had just finished showing some of my slides of a recent trip to England. One of the residents at the retirement center told me that she too had been on a journey. I was perplexed. How could this dear woman, living on a very limited income, have been on a journey? Perhaps she was remembering some trip from former years.

"You see," she said, "when Harry and I retired, we planned to travel. But then his illness took all of our savings, and we never took those trips. Now he is gone, but I still travel."

"I am not sure what you mean," I said.

She replied, "My trips are within myself. I spend a lot of time recalling my past, and reflecting on what life has meant to me. I know there is nothing left except what I keep alive within me."

What a beautiful spirit! Like the ancient psalmist she journeyed through the past in her mind and remembered the years long ago. How important to store up those memories while we are able! How much it means to "call to mind the deeds of the Lord" and to "remember thy wonders of old" (Psalm 77:11, RSV). Her disappointment at never making those "retirement trips" had become God's appointment of journeys in her mind by which she enriched her later years.

PRAYER

God, we cannot hide our fears from you, and we do fear aging and the end of this life. Only as we accept our own aging can we really hear and support others. Help our unbelief. *Amen.*

129

Your beauty should not come from outward adornment, . . . It should be that of your inner self, the unfading beauty of a gentle and quiet spirit, which is of great worth in God's sight.

1 Peter 3:3-4 (NIV)

READ FOR REFLECTION

"I try to figure out what my life has been, who I am really. That's one of the reasons I read all this psychology. So, even at my age, I haven't given up the idea that I ought to continue hunting for something valuable, and perhaps that something is my own secret self. . . ."

"My secret self, I suppose, is what someone else might call his [or her] soul. It makes me laugh, you know, thinking that when I die my soul will go somewhere, or stay somewhere, with me, or near me, or God knows where it will go. But who's to say my own little private secret soul isn't made up of all these people and things I've experienced over the years? Who's to say the soul isn't anything but secret human memory, even memory of things we wished had happened or hadn't happened to us? Who is about to educate me on *that* one?"

HELEN STANKOWSKI (a pseudonym)
as interviewed by Thomas J. Cottle

MEDITATION

The Beauty of a Mature Soul

I needed counsel. I needed someone to listen to me who could be fair and objective. I went to a friend of many years, a dear lady past seventy, and asked for her attention. She listened, and when she spoke, it was with words of wisdom. She helped me clarify the issues, sort out my feelings, and move to a decision. She got involved with my concerns but she never told me what to do.

I thought to myself as I left her home, *What a wealth of wisdom and help is neglected when we don't seek the counsel of older people.* She had a beauty of soul that touched me. I deeply respected her opinion and her mature judgment. She did not disappoint me.

Peter was right, "The unfading beauty of a gentle and quiet spirit . . . is of great worth in God's sight." Could it be that we would live healthier, less stressful lives if we sought out older people more often for friendship and counsel? Could it be that we might then better appreciate what real beauty is?

PRAYER ━━━━━━━━━━━━━━━━━━━━━━━━━━━

Creator of goodness and beauty, help our beauty not to consist of charm and cosmetics but of kindness, love, and compassion. May our clothing be your strength and dignity. *Amen.*

Ultimate Thoughts

To enter the country of age is a new experience, different from what you supposed it to be. Nobody . . . knows the country until {that person} has lived in it and has taken out . . . citizenship papers.

Malcolm Cowley

53

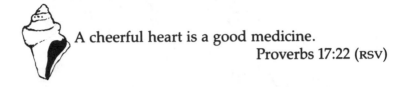 A cheerful heart is a good medicine.

Proverbs 17:22 (RSV)

READ FOR REFLECTION

Because humor brings us back to earth, it helps us to use well what is left to us even when we are keenly aware of what we have lost or been denied. Only those who know how to weep can also laugh heartily; the pain of tragedy is preparation for the depth and breadth of comedy. Sarah's laughter has this quality; as we listen with her at the entrance to the tent, we are aware of the years of waiting and stigma she has experienced. As a man in his nineties once said to me: "I used to sing and laugh a lot when I was a child. Now I am coming back around to that place again, but with a difference. I laugh now in spite of all the pain I have known."

KATHLEEN R. FISCHER

MEDITATION

God's Medicare

She was reading Psalm 1 at a seniors' Bible study at the church. She had been a diabetic for years and took medication daily. When she read verse 2, she said, "And on his law he *medicated* day and night." "Reminds me of the old man who said that cataracts were in the Bible!" one lady exclaimed. In Psalm 42:7 we read that "Deep calls to deep at the thunder of thy *cataracts*" (RSV).

I think that as I grow older there is nothing more important than a good laugh. There seems to be a link among laughter, health, and creativity. Humor relieves tension and gives us a state of well-being that lasts all day. My father kept his captivating sense of humor until the day he died, and after his death all the family wanted that little black book of his jokes.

Abraham and Sarah really thought the Lord was joking when they were told they would have a child in later life. The years had about run out on the promise that they would become parents of many nations. They learned that it was no joke—God uses older people to fulfill God's promises. When the time came, they named their son Isaac, "God has made laughter for me" (Gen. 21:6 RSV).

Laughter is "God's medicare." It is good medicine for the spirit. The ancient writer of Proverbs realized that "A cheerful heart is a good medicine." So, have a good laugh every day.

PRAYER

There is a time to mourn and a time to laugh. Help us, Source of all joy, to chuckle today over some incident or some story we hear. Let there always be the sound of laughter in our lives. *Amen.*

135

54

 A good name is more desirable than great riches;
to be esteemed is better than silver or gold.
Proverbs 22:1 (NIV)

READ FOR REFLECTION

It is indeed the task of everyone who cares to prevent people—young, middle-aged, and old—from clinging to false expectations and from building their lives on false suppositions. If it is true that people age the way they live, our first task is to help people discover life styles in which "being" is not identified with "having," self-esteem does not depend on success, and goodness is not the same as popularity. Care for the aging means a persistent refusal to attach any kind of ultimate significance to grades, degrees, positions, promotions, or rewards, and the courageous effort to keep men and women in contact with their inner self, where they can experience their own solitude and silence as potential recipients of the light. When one has not discovered and experienced the light that is love, peace, forgiveness, gentleness, kindness, and deep joy in the early years, how can one expect to recognize it in old age? As the book of Sirach says: "If you have gathered nothing in your youth, how can you find anything in your old age?" (Si 25:3-4) That is true not only of money and material goods, but also of peace and purity of heart.

HENRI J. M. NOUWEN

MEDITATION

All That Matters

What is the best legacy we can leave the next generations? We usually think of material possessions we bequeath to our family, but is that the best legacy we leave? Does this kind of gift betray our preoccupation with material things?

The accepted view today is that one *is* what one *does* or *has*, that the basis of one's value is what one produces or contributes, always measured by some material standard. The writer of Proverbs thought that "a good name" was to be chosen over material things. Character cannot be bought or easily required. It results from a life well lived.

Jesus surely left the disciples nothing of this world's goods. He died a pauper and was buried in a borrowed tomb. Yet, he left us his peace and the gift of his life.

It really matters what "name" we leave our children and grandchildren. As they remember us, what matters is how we lived, not what we acquired or what we did.

PRAYER ━━━━━━━━━━━━━━━━━━━━━━━

God of every good, help us live this day in such a way that our children and grandchildren would be proud of our name. Let our lives reflect the fruit of the Spirit: love, joy, peace, patience, kindness, goodness, faithfulness, gentleness, self-control (Gal. 5:22-23). *Amen.*

55

 God does not see as human beings see; they look at appearances but Yahweh looks at the heart.

1 Samuel 16:7 (NJB)

READ FOR REFLECTION

If an old man sees that you are really interested in his personal life, you will see a wonderful transformation take place in him. His eyes that seemed dull will light up with a new fire; his face will come alive with unexpected emotion. He . . . comes to life again, becomes a person once more. Just like the child, the old man needs to be spoken to and listened to in order to become a person, to become aware of himself, to live and grow. You will have brought about something that no social service can ever do of itself; you will have promoted him to the rank of person.

PAUL TOURNIER

MEDITATION

Now We See Clearly

What do people see when they look at an older person? White hair? A wrinkled face? Do they see that person as a mere shadow of what he or she was in younger days?

When Samuel went to the house of Jesse to anoint the new king of Israel, he looked at the sons of Jesse. Seven sons passed before him, but none was God's choice. Finally, they sent for the youngest and least eligible, David; and *he* was God's choice. Samuel had looked at the outward appearance, but the Lord knew what was in David's heart.

If you walk through a nursing home and wave or speak to people in their rooms, their faces will light up. A wonderful transformation takes place. Someone sees them. Someone pays attention to them. Someone cares.

Isn't that how Jesus treated people? He saw Zacchaeus in a tree; he heard the cries of the blind Bartimaeus; he saw the heart of the Samaritan woman at the well. And he responded to each of them. Let us, too, look beyond the outward appearance of someone to the inner person.

PRAYER

Light of all seeing, help us to look beyond appearances to the real person. May other people really "see" us, and may we, in turn, take a second look at others. Give us the eyes of Christ. *Amen.*

56

 Surely goodness and mercy shall follow me
all the days of my life;
and I shall dwell in the house of the Lord
for ever.

Psalm 23:6 (RSV)

READ FOR REFLECTION

HOW OLD ARE YOU?

Age is a quality of mind.
If you have left your dreams behind,
If hope is cold.
If you no longer look ahead,
If your ambitions' fires are dead—
Then you are old.

But if from life you take the best,
And if in life you keep the jest,
If love you hold;
No matter how the years go by,
No matter how the birthdays fly—
You are not old.

H. S. FRITSCH

MEDITATION

How Old Are You?

How old are you? Our first response is to state our age in years (although some of us are still hesitant to tell our age). Yet some of the oldest-acting people I know are young in years, and some of the most youthful people may be past sixty years of age.

David was an older man when he wrote Psalm 23, which is a kind of life review of Israel's greatest king. In it David remembered his youthful days as a shepherd and those mid-life crises which thrust him into "the valley of the shadows." But as he thought about his later years, he had a positive attitude. "Surely goodness and mercy shall follow me / all the days of my life; / and I shall dwell in the house of the Lord / for ever."

How old are you? Isn't it sad when someone says of another person, "She looks a lot older than her age"? What medical people call "secondary aging" comes about by the effect of stress on us in earlier years. But as long as we "fight the good fight, and keep the faith," we can be like those written of in the Book of Proverbs, "The path of the righteous is like the light of dawn, / which shines brighter and brighter until full day" (Prov. 4:18, RSV).

How old are you? Instead of revealing your age in clock time, let your life show your age. "Let your light so shine before men, that they may see your good works and glorify your Father in heaven" (Matt. 5:16, NKJV).

PRAYER

God of the beginning, God of the end, help us to count our years not by how long we have lived, but by how well we have lived. May we never give up our dreams or surrender the fight but remain faithful until life's end. *Amen.*

Hence I remind you to rekindle the gift of God that is within you.

2 Timothy 1:6 (RSV)

READ FOR REFLECTION

I have associated creativity and spirituality as being initially present in early childhood and then being largely ignored by the adult world and education—to reappear at least in some people in old age. . . .

We tend to think of higher creativity or genius as something reserved for a few highly gifted people whom we can only admire or envy. There is a growing awareness that we may all have such latent potential, but that we reject the possibility without ever considering it seriously. It may be that the elderly in some instances, freed from the restraints of a routine job and caring less about appearances and the inhibitions imposed by our culture, are in a position to contemplate the meaning of life. If so, they may look inward and discover other more spiritual, intuitive, inspirational or creative ideas.

MAXWELL JONES

MEDITATION

Stir Up the Gift of God within You

The two-talent person was commended for his faithfulness, not his brilliance. He received the same reward as the five-talent person. Every one of us has unique talents and gifts in old age. The question is: Will we use them or lose them? Retirement presents an unparalleled opportunity to develop latent talents. Some of the greatest works in the arts, literature, and other fields have come from persons past seventy.

It is easier to grow old if we are neither bored nor boring. Projects are vital to our mental health, and there is no limit to realizing our potential. In our later years we have more time to expand our horizons because we are set free from certain routines and rituals.

The problem is often within us. We are locked in a room with open doors. We try to blame our boredom on outside forces, but the issue is within us. If we take the time to look inward, we may be surprised at our own creativity and ingenuity. Who knows? We may even experience a rebirth of creativity in later years—and amaze ourselves with our newfound gifts.

PRAYER

Generous Provider of all good gifts, rekindle within us latent and buried talents so often neglected in earlier life. May we find in older age the creative persons you always knew us to be. *Amen.*

143

Therefore, since we are surrounded by so great a cloud of witnesses, let us lay aside every weight, . . . and let us run with perseverance the race that is set before us.

Hebrews 12:1 (RSV)

READ FOR REFLECTION

In *The Sacred Journey*, Frederick Buechner stresses that we can continue to learn from all of our memories. Memory, he says, is not the looking back to a past that no longer exists. Rather, it allows us to look into an altogether new kind of time where everything that ever was continues to be. Something of the power and richness of life continues to touch us through the people we loved and who loved us, the people who taught us things: "Dead and gone though they may be, as we come to understand them in new ways, it is as though they come to understand us—and through them we come to understand ourselves—in new ways too." This, Buechner believes, is something of the meaning of the communion of saints.

KATHLEEN R. FISCHER

MEDITATION

New Meaning from an Old Creed

Older people in my parish tell me that the Lord's Supper becomes more meaningful to them as life moves on. One of the reasons is that when they come to the Lord's table they feel the presence of family and friends who have died in the faith. This is new insight into the words of the old creed: *I believe in . . . the communion of saints.*

Whatever else that phrase means, it affirms belief in the union of all true believers in all ages past and in the future ages to come. The familiar anthem of the New Orleans jazz funeral catches up the whole idea, "Oh, when the saints go marching in . . . O Lord, I want to be in that number, when the saints go marching in."

Not only do the faithful of the past live in our memories, but we also live in theirs. The "communion of saints" means that those who have finished the course in faith—the "cloud of witnesses"—who now rest from their labors are not separated from us.

They are the "fans in the stands" who cheer us on, as we run the same race set before us. Isn't it comforting to know we are not alone in the Christian life, but we are surrounded and undergirded by such a supporting cast!

PRAYER ━━━━━━━━━━━━━━━━━━━━━━━━━

Loving Lord, for the genuine feeling of support and encouragement offered us by the faithful saints of the past, we thank you. Now help us to run the race with perseverance, so we too may join the community of saints. *Amen.*

Blessed be the God and Father of our Lord Jesus Christ . . . who comforts us in all our affliction, so that we may be able to comfort those who are in any affliction, with the comfort with which we ourselves are comforted by God.

2 Corinthians 1:3-4 (RSV)

READ FOR REFLECTION

Psychological healing of one's own spirit requires an energetic but faith-filled encounter with personal wounds. Our physical and mental hurts can become teachers of understanding and empathy. Scholars have noted the gerontomorphic images of God in our cultural tradition, that is, God portrayed in the figure of an old man. God or the gods are described as old, wise, and powerful. Simmons speculates that the old have traditionally been the custodians of religion, and thus have shaped positive pictures of divinity in their own best images. A more authentic image of God in the guise of the old, however, is that of a wounded healer, of one who has suffered the wounds of life's ages, whose wisdom and mercy are healing precisely because these qualities have been forged in the crucible of the world's suffering.

The elder as wounded healer can be seen living out a most productive part of life.

EUGENE C. BIANCHI

MEDITATION

Wounded Healers

Older people have wounds. You cannot live in this world without experiencing some brokenness and weakness. Our wounds can become a source of healing for others. This does not mean that we dwell on our problems, or tell everyone about our ills. Look to Christ as the wounded healer. "By his wounds we are healed" (Isa. 53:5, NIV) said the ancient prophet of the Messiah, and Jesus fulfilled those words with his life and suffering. "He was wounded for our transgressions" (Isa. 53:5, RSV). His pain became the place where healing and power become available.

Older people can be wounded healers. Who really helps us? Someone who answers all our questions? Someone who solves our problems or gives us advice? No, it is the person who gently binds up our wounds and who stands with us with a calm presence. It is someone who is not scared by the silence of our despair or frightened by absorbing our distress.

Our weakness, then, can be a blessing to someone else. Our infirmities and our comfort can minister to others. Older people can be God's wounded healers.

PRAYER ═══════════════════════════════

God of remembrance, help us remember moments of weakness in our lives and how we were comforted; then may we reach out to others and may our wounds be a help in their healing. *Amen.*

147

60

 Truly, I say to you, unless you turn and become like children, you will never enter the kingdom of heaven.

Matthew 18:3 (RSV)

READ FOR REFLECTION

The purpose of our personal universe is the unceasing expansion of our personal awareness. When we are on this road we are in harmony with ourselves, our companions, and the universe. By simply continuing to learn—and learn about things that naturally interest us—we are forever experiencing fulfillment rather than frustration. Boredom vanishes, depression evaporates, and a new, ever expanding, noncompetitive universe opens up. We have found our own "preventive/supportive measures." All that is required is to reactivate the same alert curious mind that has been ours from the beginning and reopen avenues of inquiry we had long ago felt obliged to close because of the pressure of circumstances.

JEROME ELLISON

MEDITATION

Never Too Old to Learn

Second childhood is a phrase traditionally used to indicate senility. Older people are accused of being in their "second childhood" when they clamor for attention or act in a forgetful manner. But "second childhood" can mean an alert, experimenting mind.

When Jesus told the disciples, "Unless you turn and become like children, you will never enter the kingdom of heaven," he meant that in a child we see the characteristics of the kingdom. A child's humility, trust, and dependence are all qualities of the kingdom. A child's natural curiosity and ability to wonder is another.

Little children have a love affair with life and are curious about the world they live in. Watching them learn is a fascinating experience. They are full of questions and never stop begging for answers.

We should be like little children in our love of learning. Perhaps we need to consider enrolling in an adult education course, attend an Elderhostel program, or join a special interest group. So, enjoy that "second childhood."

PRAYER

Eternal Source of knowledge, help us realize that the life of the mind is the service of God and that we can learn as long as we live. *Amen.*

61

 So faith, hope, love abide, these three; but the greatest of these is love.

1 Corinthians 13:13 (RSV)

READ FOR REFLECTION

You will find as you look back upon your life that the moments that stand out, the moments when you have really lived, are the moments when you have done things in a spirit of love. As memory scans the past, above and beyond all transitory pleasures of life, there leap forward those supreme hours when you have been enabled to do unnoticed kindnesses to those around you, things too trifling to speak about, but which you feel have entered into your eternal life. I have seen almost all the beautiful things that God has made; I have enjoyed almost every pleasure that [God] has planned for [people]; and yet as I look back I see standing out above all the life that has gone four or five short experiences when the love of God reflected itself in some poor imitation, some small act of love of mine, and these seem to be things which alone of all one's life abide. Everything else in all our lives is transitory. Every other good is visionary. But the acts of love which no [one] knows about, or can ever know about—they never fail.

HENRY DRUMMOND

MEDITATION

Love Is the Last Word

Whether it is early or late in life, the greatest thing in the world is Christian love. Looking back on our lives, what we remember are those precious moments when someone loved us—truly loved us—or when that love broke through us to others.

Henry Drummond has said, "As I look back I see standing out above all the life that has gone four or five short experiences when the love of God reflected itself in some poor imitation, some small act of love of mine, and these seem to be things which alone of all one's life abide." Older people can attest to the truth of these words. Love alone lasts.

Older people know the reality of love's eminence. They are no longer deceived or fooled by sham or pretense. They know when someone really cares for them, bears with their infirmities, ministers to their needs. Faith and hope are magnificent virtues. But the greatest of these is love. Love never fails. It is the ultimate word.

PRAYER

Lover of souls, for those persons who have really loved us and have shown us your love in this life, we thank you. The only way we can thank them or you is to pass that love on to others. *Amen.*

62

Read John 2:1-11

 The steward said, "Everyone brings out the choice wine first and then the cheaper wine after the guests have had too much to drink; but you have saved the best till now."

John 2:10 (NIV)

READ FOR REFLECTION

What we ask of life is that we may be set free from certain forms of service, not for idleness, but that we may do less in order to the doing of more; in order that we may employ the great gains that the years have brought to us in the interest of our fellow [human beings]; in order that with increasing faith we may encourage dawning faith; in order that with more patient hope we may recover hope when it fades in the lives of others; in order that with developed and enlarged love, we may provide a refuge for those who need our help.

I suppose it would be impossible for anyone familiar with Browning to think along these lines without finding his words singing themselves in his soul again.

Grow old along with me!
The best is yet to be,
The last of life, for which the first was made.

Our times are in His Hand
Who saith, "A whole I planned,"
"Youth shows but half; trust God, see all, nor be
    afraid!"

G. CAMPBELL MORGAN

152

MEDITATION

Saving the Best until Last

Jesus seemed to reverse things. For him, the "first will be last, and the last first" (Matt. 19:30, RSV). His first miracle at Cana in Galilee caused the steward to tell the bridegroom, "You have kept the best wine till now."

Usually we think that the best years of our lives are earlier. College years, the first child, the excitement of success all seem our best years. But God saves the best until last. The last wine may be the most exhilarating of all, and that's food for thought.

Instead of getting depressed about growing older, we need to celebrate these last years. At the end we begin to see God's plan worked out to its fullest. To paraphrase Robert Browning, "This is the last of life, for which the first was made." Savor the last wine. It probably will be the best!

PRAYER

O God, Alpha and Omega, you created us for a reason, and now as we approach the end of life, we do so with appreciation and joy. May our last days be our best.
Amen.

Index of Biblical Passages